First published in 2019 by Achieve the Impossible Pty Ltd

ISBN-13: 978 0 6485616 9 9

Text and Cover Design by: ASMBLY

Printed and bound in Australia by Revolution Print

Disclaimer:

The material in this publication is of the nature of general comment only, and does not represent professional advice. It is not intended to provide specific guidance for particular circumstances and it should not be relied on as the basis for any decision to take action or not take action on any matter which it covers. Readers should obtain professional advice where appropriate, before making any such decision. To the maximum extent permitted by law, the author and publisher disclaim all responsibility and liability to any person, arising directly or indirectly from any person taking or not taking action based on the information in this publication.

PETER J BONE

ACHIEVE THE IMPOSSIBLE

Jasmine,

Trust this book inspires
Achieve your Impossible!

ACHIEVE THE IMPOSSIBLE

BY PETER J BONE

INTRODUCTION

I cannot believe six years after starting a little old Instagram account called 'Achieve the Impossible' that I would be holding a book that represents my impossible dream. A book that represents my heart, dreams and passions to inspire, challenge and equip you to achieve your impossible dreams.

I've written this book for you.

Yes...YOU!

This book is for you!

Because it's for you, I'm speaking directly to you.

But I don't want these words to hit your brain and then bounce off. I'm not interested in your mind trying to figure out what makes sense.

I'm writing to something much more powerful than your mind. I'm writing to your heart.

Your heart has your impossible dream locked up within. Your heart holds the unseen desires of your future. Your heart is what's going to fuel this journey to your impossible dream!

Not to sound rude, but your mind simply cannot comprehend the details of the impossible. It can't plot and plan out every single step in the future to take you to your impossible dream. It's just not created that way.

But your heart can.

That's because your heart represents you.

Your heart holds the map to the journey ahead. Your head can see where you are now and where you want to be, but only your heart truly has access to the steps that make up this journey.

Your impossible dream can be achieved as you become the person who can achieve it, one step at a time.

This isn't about knowledge as much as it is about faith, hope and trust.

I write from a place of a personal faith in Jesus Christ, but my writing isn't just for people who believe what I believe.

I wrote this book for anyone who believes in their impossible dream. You don't have to know the details of the future, because, to be honest, none of us do.

If that were the case, this book would be read by absolutely no one.

This book is for people who believe that every day on earth is another opportunity to step closer to achieving what once seemed impossible.

I've written this book as a series of small chapters to be ingested daily. This book is designed to be used as a daily source of inspiration, to represent ideas, concepts and my obvious obsession with metaphors and picture-words that I know can equip you to achieve your impossible dreams.

Take your time on each chapter. Though small, they pack a powerful punch when applied to a daily life.

I trust this book inspires, challenges and equips you on the journey to your impossible dreams.

STORY BEHIND ACHIEVE THE IMPOSSIBLE

In late November 2013, in our family home on the Sunshine Coast of Australia, I was told the news no son ever wants to hear. I was asked to take a seat in the living room as my Mother and Father bravely told me that Dad had just been diagnosed with terminal cancer.

This came as an absolute shock to me and my very close family, and was only discovered after a routine blood test. I had grown up with illustrious dreams and visions of how I would honour my parents' legacy by purchasing them a house, allowing them to enjoy their retirement without the worry of finances hovering over their heads.

They had both worked so hard their entire lives, and deserved nothing less than to be rewarded for their incredibly generous and selfless lives. The news of Dad's cancer was the needle to my balloon of dreams, exploding right before me.

I honestly thought I had years and years ahead of me that I could find a way to provide for the most incredible parents in the world, and to give back after all they had given me and my two older brothers. I was wrong.

Moments like this have their way of piercing through all of the day-to-day worries and issues that life brings and really bring immense clarity and purpose as to what really matters in this world.

It was in quiet reflection time that I began to question what I had been doing with the life I had been given, and what I was doing to be the very best version of myself that I could possibly be.

I was living a very comfortable lifestyle, with great people around me, a nice house and a beautiful car (my pride and joy, something Dad was especially proud of). This forced me to answer a question that was always in the back of my mind, but never really made it consistently past my thoughts into action territory, where I'd actually do something about it.

Was I really living life to its fullest potential? Am I using the gifts and talents I have been blessed with to the very best of my ability, to create the most amazing life for myself, the people closest to me and society?

I had a serious little chat to myself and decided to go out and take hold of my future, taking action to achieve the goals and dreams I had set for myself and been planning and thinking about for years. It's not until you realize that action is required to turn your dreams into reality that you start to take your responsibilities seriously.

I had the responsibility to bring my dreams from the intangible, unseen realms of my heart, mind and soul, out into the world around me. And the only way that could be done was through action.

One of my dreams had always been to inspire people to achieve their greatest potential. The issue I kept telling myself was that I didn't know exactly how I was going to do that.

I would work alongside those closest to me and have inspirational coffee catch-ups where we spent time dreaming, planning and setting goals. I told myself this was all I needed to do to keep my passion flickering for inspiring others, and continued this mediocre way of living until news of Dad's illness forced me to take action. Not just any action...BIG action!

On the 13th December 2013, I set up an Instagram account called 'achievetheimpossible'. I had no idea what I was doing, what I intended doing, or even what I was meant to be doing.

But I was doing. And that was the key, DOING. I had taken the first steps of action in expanding my dream of inspiring others. I began posting quotes that inspired me, hoping they would resound and inspire others as they have inspired me - it seemed like a good fit. I loved being inspired, and now I can share that passion with others.

The success from that one decision to start has far exceeded anything I could of ever imagined... I naturally try to think big, but the way the account has been received by incredible, like-minded followers has been truly outstanding, and inspires me everyday to grow it to a wider audience with the purpose to inspire!

Today, we are reaching over a million people from all different walks from all around the world. That is something my mind cannot fathom, but is so grateful for.

Five years on, as I sit writing this book, I realise I am doing the exact same thing I did setting up @achievetheimpossible.

I am taking a leap of faith, not knowing exactly what I am doing, but knowing for certain that I am meant to be doing it. Taking action feels fantastic!

So, I welcome you on this journey of the 'Achieve the Impossible Book'.

I trust and pray it blesses, inspires, challenges and encourages you to reach your potential and most importantly, achieve your impossible.

Peter J. Bone

CONTENTS

SELF-BELIEF

Choose to listen to the voice of hope and the opinions of those who matter.

ACHIEVETHEIMPOSSIBLE

SELF TALK TO SUCCESS

Achieving the Impossible is all about the journey to our impossible dreams.

We know that there is substantial distance between your current location and your final destination. We also know that until time travel is invented, travelling this distance is going to require time.

What better way to start the book than by spending quality time together. Time for a roadtrip! Before we embark, we've got to prepare. Now, after we've checked the car and filled the tank, there is one vital thing to check off the list before we continue any further on this journey.

What we are listening to...the roadtrip playlist!

Now I'm not necessarily talking about the songs we're gonna play on the way. On an actual roadtrip, anyone who knows me, knows this would obviously be of the utmost importance.

In Pete's weird metaphor roadtrip you're now a part of, we are talking about the voices, opinions and thoughts we are listening to for the journey ahead.

Who knows a playlist has the power to completely make or break a great roadtrip?!

You can either be belting out a banger of a sing-a-long at the top of your lungs or awkwardly hiding back in your seat, hoping to be sucked in the spongey safety of obscurity.

The great thing about the journey to your impossible dream is you are connected to your car's Bluetooth. You have control and the final say on what gets played!

On our phones, we have access to all sorts of music; happy songs, sad songs, and everything in between. All could have their time and place if that's what you're in to.

Even though you have access to every song on the planet on your device, what you choose to listen to is completely up to you.

Are you going to listen to the negative opinion of someone you went to school with in 1973 or that still small voice of hope within your soul?

Are you choosing to listen to that opinion of a close friend who thinks you're crazy for what you're trying to do, or listen to your heart that knows your family's future legacy depends on this journey?

Are you going to listen to your own negative, self-doubting and over-thinking voices, or choose to shut them up and focus on the possibilities through the lens of faith and trust?

The things you choose to listen to are going to determine how enjoyable the journey is, and very possibly, how far you go.

Choose to listen to the voice of hope and the opinions of those who matter.

Look at your journey through the lens of faith and trust, and no matter what others may say, believe in yourself and your seemingly impossible dreams.

You've got them for a reason. Make the choice to listen to them.

Believe in your dreams.

The seeds in your field are there because that's the perfect place for them to grow!

ACHIEVETHEIMPOSSIBLE

IT IS YOURS

If God wants you to have it, the blessing will forever have your name on it. That's why it's important not to over-think or question the way things unfold in your life.

Ok, I'm gonna be completely real and vulnerable with you for a moment here. Over-thinking is something I do extremely well.

Me and my fellow over-thinkers know what it's like walking away from a conversation replaying every facial expression, then moving on to question the tone, the intent, even the motive behind what feels like every second word!

Now, prepare yourself for one of my famous metaphor picture-word thingys. My followers on Instagram are definitely used to them and I'm sure you'll learn to love them over here in the world of a physical book too!

Over-thinking sows the seeds of doubt in an otherwise perfectly normal situation.

We can begin to question what we have experienced and become insecure in our beliefs and thoughts.

Just as in an everyday conversation, all of us can fall into the trap of over-thinking when it comes to our dreams, desires, ambitions and destiny.

Now, this is not to be mixed up with merely thinking about them. Trust me, that's a good thing and will get you on the right track to achieving those dreams of yours!

The issue rises when we start to feed those doubts and fears by over-thinking.

We'll ask ourselves questions like:

'Am I good enough?'

'Does anybody even care?'

'Who am I to do this?'

'What will happen if this dream does come true?'

'Could I even handle it?'

'Is it really for me?'

These questions will always pop up in our dreams whenever we are pursuing something that seems 'impossible'.

Fears and doubts are natural. But they are like weeds.

Their sole purpose is to strangle the healthy plants representing your passion and purpose that can grow strong and eventually bring your dreams into reality.

These weedy doubts and fears have the power to suck the life out of our potential.

BUT...we have control over those thoughts!

We can choose to focus on the weeds, and unintentionally water them by over-thinking, or we can see them for what they really are and actively remove them from our field of dreams.

God has planted those seeds in your heart for a reason.

Your field is the perfect place for those seeds representing your dreams, desires and ambitions to flourish.

Let's not allow weeds to take root and grow by over-thinking.

So next time you see a weed pop up, make the choice, take action and pull it out.

Don't water it by over-thinking and focusing your attention on your doubts and fears.

Trust you've got your dreams for a reason.

Believe in yourself and your dreams. The seeds in your field are there because that's the perfect place for them to grow!

Stop stressing over where you've been and start trusting where you're going.

Your future starts now.

ACHIEVETHEIMPOSSIBLE

YOU'RE STILL YOUNG

Daily reminder...You're still young and not supposed to have your whole life figured out just yet. Everything will work out. Stop stressing and start trusting.

I don't know about you, but for me those first two words hold just as much power as the rest of the quote. 'Daily Reminder...'

We live in a world that's as busy as ever.

Every single day, you and I are surrounded by messages, expectations and opinions of society, ourselves and those closest to us.

There's not a lot we can change that we have absolute direct control over. But there is definitely something we can control and have direct influence over... what we are filling our minds with.

Are you creating a positive space where you allow your un-birthed dreams, desires and ambitions to flourish?

Or are the pressures and weight of the world blowing out that flickering flame within?

From today onwards, I'd like you to be intentional about feeding your mind positive thoughts.

It sounds easy, but this isn't always the case.

Positive, life-giving thoughts and opinions don't necessarily come naturally by society or even ourselves. We really do need to be intentional about our attitude and perspective towards the thoughts we choose to hold on to.

Is it going to be...

'You're right...I'm not good enough. I'll never be able to do that.'

OR...

'I know I'm not where I want to be just yet. But I also know I'm not where I once was. I am on the journey of becoming the person my impossible dreams need me to be.'

It seems to be 1000x harder (not a scientifically proven number, sorry!) to create the habit of flipping those negative thoughts into positive affirmations.

This transformation in thoughts doesn't change where you are in this very moment in time. They don't magically change your reality or where you're standing.

But what they do change is the direction you're facing.

That direction is where you're heading the moment you take your next step.

Whether you realize it or not, you're taking that step today.

You might not be where you want to be, but you aren't where you were.

When you're facing the right direction and taking daily steps towards your dreams, time becomes your greatest asset.

When today's quote says 'you're still young...' I can hear some of you saying 'I'm in my 60's! I'm not young! (shoutout to my amazing Mum, who I'm sure will be one of the first people reading this.)

Are you comparing your age to the rest of the world through the lens of their expectations? Or are you comparing it to the direction you're facing?

Because when you're facing the right direction, the moment you take that step is the moment your future starts.

Why don't we start comparing our age in relation to our future? Everything can change when we realize we're as young today as we'll ever be.

We won't know the exact intricate details of our journey ahead, but what we do know is when we are facing the right direction and taking daily steps in the direction of our dreams, the best is yet to come.

Stop stressing over where you've been and start trusting where you're going. Your future starts now.

You have one life.
Live it!

ACHIEVETHEIMPOSSIBLE

ONE LIFE

Are there two words that could motivate you to pursue you goals, ambitions and dreams more than this?! We have ONE LIFE. The odds of you being born are something like 400 TRILLION to ONE!

The fact that you are alive, breathing and reading this is an incredible accomplishment. We've been created and chosen to live right now!

With this one life we all have, I urge you, no, I BEG you, make the very most of it.

If you're not happy with something, change it. If you don't have healthy, supportive relationships, change them.

If you're not where you want to be, change. Change your environment, change your people, change your mindset.

We simply can not get to the end of our time on earth and wonder 'what if?' Let's make a stand today and start living an intentional life; a life where we go out of our way to love those around us, a life where we respect the power of our dreams, a life where we use what we have to get to where we want to be!

We only live once? Wrong. We only die once.

We live EVERY DAY.

We have one life. Please, I beg of you, make it count.

Allow the pain of regret to guide you out of your comfort zone.

ACHIEVETHEIMPOSSIBLE

REGRET INTO RESPONSE

Don't regret the things you've done. Regret the things you didn't do when you had the chance.

I had a conversation with someone a couple of days ago that has really stuck with me. This entrepreneur was unsure whether to go all in on their passion and purpose, leave the safety and security of their corporate job and start something new aligned with their dreams.

Amongst the nuggets of wisdom I tried to share, one thought cut through and took hold in this person's life. I merely asked the following question...

'If you looked back a year from now, would you regret not taking the chance on your dreams?'

This is the central focus of this chapter.

Harness the pain of future regret.

Let the potential pain of not taking the chance push you into making a decision.

Change is scary.

Change is daunting.

But change is essential.

Three and a half years ago, I had to make the decision to leave my comfortable Teaching job to pursue my impossible dreams.

I had an amazing job and worked with amazing people; I could've happily continued working there and lived a comfortable life.

But when you've got an opportunity to take a leap that gets you closer to your dreams, your passion and your purpose, you've just gotta jump!

I was faced with two paths; the well-travelled 'comfortable' teaching job, or the unknown path of social media.

It came down to one single question - 'In a year from now, will I regret not taking this opportunity?' Something stirred in my heart, and even though I had no guarantee, it just felt like that was the thing I had to do.

For me personally, I allowed the potential pain of regret to fuel one of the bravest decisions I've ever made in my life.

What chances and opportunities are coming your way? Ask yourself if you'll regret not taking them a year from now, let alone ten years.

Allow the pain of that regret to guide you out of your comfort zone.

You lack nothing.
Use what God gave you.

ACHIEVETHEIMPOSSIBLE

YOU LACK NOTHING

You lack nothing. Use what God gave you.

Let's talk about the flames of your impossible dream.

Some of you may be at the stage where you've got a small flickering flame within and searching for the right time to stoke those flames and add fuel to it.

Others may be on the hunt to actually find that flame and be willing to spark it by striking PASSION and PREPARATION together.

There will also be those of you who are actively listening to your gut instincts, discerning your next step that will fan your flames.

No matter the stage of your journey you are in right now, it can be a daunting prospect when we consider where we are in relation to where our dreams need us to be.

Feelings of insecurity, fear of the unknown and worries of inadequacy all create doubts which can affect our self-worth, self-identity and our journey ahead.

I wanna take a moment to speak into those potentially dream-smothering feelings right now.

You lack nothing. Use what God gave you.

As I mentioned earlier in the book, God doesn't go around and throw dreams around at random. He gives them to people along with a specific set of gifts, talents and abilities needed to make that dream come true.

Are these God-given gifts in their final, complete and perfected state? Absolutely not.

You have been personally given them with the goal of developing those gifts to a stage where they can be used to help achieve that impossible dream of yours.

Trust in what you've been given.

Batteries are pretty useless by themselves, but when they accompany a Remote Control car, they have the power to bring that chunk of plastic and rubber to life!

You've been given your remote control car.

You've also been given the batteries to bring it to life and help it achieve its purpose.

Put the two together and watch as you confidently journey step by step towards your impossible dream!

Just because it hasn't arrived yet, doesn't mean it's not on its way.

ACHIEVETHEIMPOSSIBLE

PATIENCE AND BELIEF

We're on the journey to our impossible dreams.

Step by step, we continue on the path we feel has our name on it. As we walk along this journey, we will experience uphill challenges and downhill rewards.

These moments show a sense of momentum and traction required for progress.

But what happens when we filter the extremes out of our journey and focus on the remaining majority which is often reasonably level and can be uneventful, even somewhat mundane?

What do we do when our dreams seem like they're taking forever?

Two words. Patience and Belief.

Patience

Patience is not simply passively walking around waiting for opportunities and the right moment.

Patience is about actively pursuing the moment, whilst trusting in the outcome and results.

Let's not try and rush the journey (even those mundane parts that seem like they're taking forever!) There are things we need to pick up and learn along the way to the more glorified and eventful highs and lows ahead.

Patience is about making the most of every moment.

Doing everything you can within the NOW moment you've been given and trust in the outcome and result of what's NEXT.

Belief

When the path ahead isn't clear or the storms of life are restricting your vision, it's important to know what to hold onto to maintain your balance and sense of direction on your impossible journey.

Belief in your impossible dream says even when I can't see the destination or even the exact steps ahead, I have faith and trust this is my path.

Belief is important when you can see where you are going, but becomes vital when you are approaching a challenge or when the road ahead becomes slippery or uneven.

It's easy to fall into fear and doubt and allow our belief to slide.

Stabilize your feet with belief, that belief in your path and your God-given passion and purpose.

Sometimes you've got to walk towards your blessings to claim them. Other times, be still. Have patience and belief and be prepared to receive those blessings.

When the thoughts of doubt and fear come into your life, have patience and belief in your path and the journey ahead. There will be times where you're not making the progress you expected, but know one thing...your blessings are on their way!

Tomorrow's success is relying on today's watering of the seeds of yesterday's planting.

ACHIEVETHEIMPOSSIBLE

BELIEVE IN YOUR BAMBOO

Believe in yourself and all that you are. Know that there is something inside you that is greater than any obstacle.

There's a story I heard a few years ago that has stuck with me every time I start to worry about, doubt or question the timing of something I've expected to happen in my life.

It's a true story that is found in nature and perfectly reflects faith in the unseen.

Stronger per inch than concrete, the Chinese Bamboo Tree has incredible potential and is renowned for its strength, durability and flexibility.

When planted however, this tree shows absolutely no sign of growth or progress.

One month passes...nothing.

Three months pass...still nothing.

Twelve months...nada.

Three years...nope. Still just dirt.

Five years...hold on...what's this?!

For five years, not even a sprout emerges from the soil. There are no visible signs of growth from the Chinese Bamboo Tree for over 1800 days!

However, on each of those days, because of its tough outer layer, the seed buried in the ground requires constant watering and fertilisation.

Even just a day or two without water could kill the seed.

Such consistent investment for no visible result can leave us wondering if it is even worth it.

I'm sure there has been or is something in your life right now that you're investing into without seeing any visible signs of growth or return.

The thought of giving up has crossed your mind plenty of times, but there's something on the inside of you saying 'hang in there...don't give up'.

Those farmers who don't give up and continue watering the seed of the Chinese Bamboo Tree for those five underground years bear witness to one of the most powerful forces of nature.

In the fifth year, when that sprout emerges from its burial place, the Chinese Bamboo Tree grows a massive 80 feet in a space of just six weeks!

The question is...did it grow 80 feet in six weeks or five years? The answer... of course, five years.

Tomorrow's success is relying on today's watering of the seeds of yesterday's planting. When self-doubt, disbelief and negativity creep in, think back to the Chinese Bamboo Tree.

You've planted the seeds for your impossible dream. Now it's time to water and nourish them. Some will take longer than others to emerge, but the results will end up speaking for themselves when they grow exponentially.

Believe in your dreams. Water and nourish them. You've planted them for a reason. Now prepare for unparalleled, exponential growth!

PURPOSE

Sometimes, the plans we have for life are there to get us to a checkpoint in our journey, not the final destination.

ACHIEVETHEIMPOSSIBLE

PURPOSE IN A PLAN

Our life does not always turn out the way we planned, but sometimes that's because what we planned wasn't supposed to be our life.

My 'plan' was to get married at 24.

I'm not sure whether it was just because 24 was my favorite number, or I had some inspired vision of how my life would be when I was 'all grown up', but I do know my plans haven't turned out anything like I expected them to.

A conversation with a friend a while back triggered this specific memory of marriage. No prizes for guessing, but I'm now 7yrs past what I once thought was my 'marriage use by date'.

We all have these plans in our minds.

Plans that we truly believe and put our faith in. There are times when these plans reveal themselves and life follows along with our structured ideals.

Then there are times when life throws curveballs and reality couldn't be further away from what we once swore would happen.

When life doesn't go the way we planned it, the feelings of failure, rejection and inadequacy can rear their ugly heads in our mind.

Does this mean we have failed?

Not at all.

I strongly believe that our plans, regardless of whether they succeed or fail, are necessary for the season of life we're in.

It's often when things don't go according to plan, that we learn our greatest lessons and discover our greatest breakthroughs.

I had 'planned' to go to business school before I got offered a teaching position. The skills I learnt in teaching today lay the foundation for much of my writing, coaching and speaking.

Sometimes, the plans we have for life are there to get us to a checkpoint in our journey, not the final destination.

We collect life experiences, wisdom and knowledge that we often couldn't get anywhere else. You'll find these will be essential acquisitions as you continue on your journey.

So, if your life isn't going according to plan, smile.

Take a deep breath and know that you're on the path you need to be to get you to where you need to go.

By all means, plan. Take action.

Then be prepared for changes and have the courage to adapt. Have faith in the journey. Trust the process. Achieve the impossible.

A pause produces patience and prioritizes purpose.

ACHIEVETHEIMPOSSIBLE

POWER OF A PAUSE

A Pause Produces Patience and Prioritizes Purpose.

We've all had those mornings where nothing seems to go right.

I had a morning like this recently. I woke up with a thousand things racing around my mind, a fresh surprise pile of dog vomit on the carpet right beside my bed with the leftovers on my brand new linen bed cover and a throat that really didn't want anything to do with humans today.

This is not the ideal best combo, especially when you've got to jump on a plane to Bali to use that throat to deliver a keynote followed by a full day of Instagram Workshops the day after!

Today was going to be absolutely jam-packed whether I liked it or not.

I was mildly freaking out when I reached out to a close friend who said that today I just needed to 'pause'.

PAUSE?! Pausing life sounds great when you've got nothing on your to-do list!

I looked at that monstrous to-do list for my day, which now included cleaning carpets and washing every single piece of my bedding.

I couldn't afford to 'pause'. I had too much to do.

But on the other hand, I quickly realized I couldn't afford not to pause.

I decided to try and pause.

Not the 'sit down and do nothing' type of pause.

This morning, I learnt there was another type of pause.

The pause that lets us still our crazy thoughts that are flying all around and see the day for what it is. Stop trying to chase every single moving part of the day and pause the tasks on the to-do list.

Have you ever tried to count people at a busy city intersection? Ok, I haven't either, but that's the picture I get, so we're gonna just flow with it.

These people are rushing around in all different directions trying to get from one place to their next destination.

Different angles, different directions, different speeds. And your job is to count them!

Then, to top it off, you're trying to feel more productive, so you start running in and around the people to get better angles and more of a feel of the busy crossing.

You feel busier and because you're doing more, but really in trying to do everything, you end up doing nothing.

Pausing doesn't mean giving up and stopping to a standstill.

The stop and pause button on a TV remote are very different for a reason.

When we pause, we can either pause our tasks (the people crossing the intersection) or we can pause ourselves and take stock of the things passing us.

By pausing, we are actually becoming more productive because our vantage point and our mindset are calm and at peace, which highlights our purpose and priorities.

The pause produces patience.

That patience in our purpose redirects our passion to what is the most productive use of our resources.

Next time you're counting people at a bustling city intersection or, more likely, trying to juggle your to-do lists and your emotional well-being, I encourage you to PAUSE.

A pause produces patience and prioritizes purpose.

Your world needs you to be pursuing that dream of yours, even when it seems impossible!

ACHIEVETHEIMPOSSIBLE

PASSION FUELS YOUR FUTURE

"To succeed, you have to believe in something with such a passion that it becomes a reality." - Anita Roddick

Passion sets the foundation for your purpose and sets the direction of your dreams.

Late in 2018, I spoke to a group of entrepreneurs in Bali. We discussed the importance of aligning your passion to your purpose to sustain your journey ahead.

That passion is going to be the thing that picks you up when you think you've stumbled for the last time, it's going to be the thing that puts wind back in your sails and breathes life into that dying dream.

Passion comes from a genuine and intentional sense of awareness and understanding of the WHY behind the HOW and WHAT you do.

If you're yet to discover your passion, don't worry!

You have a couple of choices, which will both require an intentional directional shift.

You can either change your circumstances or you can begin the journey of changing yourself.

I beg of you, on behalf of your untapped potential, to do everything in your power to cultivate and develop that passion within you.

Your life will start to change when that flame of passion within you is given the power to flicker. As you continue to fuel your passion, the flame burns brighter.

The brighter your inner flame shines, the more people you can reach and warmth with your passion.

Ignite that passion within!

Your dream needs you. Your world needs you to be pursuing that dream of yours, even when it seems impossible!

Cultivate that passion...it will be the fuel to sustain you on the journey to becoming the very best version of yourself!

Sometimes God will destroy your comfort to encourage you to step into your calling.

ACHIEVETHEIMPOSSIBLE

CAUGHT BY COMFORT

Being comfortable feels great.

For me personally, I love knowing exactly what I'm doing, where I'm going and how I'm going to to get there.

5 years ago, I remember telling someone how comfortable I was in my Teaching job. I knew what I was doing, I knew I was good at it, I was passionate about it and I worked alongside amazing people.

This comfort was destroyed when Mum and Dad sat me down in the family lounge room in late Nov 2013 and told me Dad had just been diagnosed with terminal Pancreatic Cancer and was given just a few short months to live.

My dreams of setting Mum and Dad up with a beautiful retirement had burst like a balloon. My comfortable lifestyle was the thing that had kept me from pursuing my 'impossible' dreams.

We can become comfortable in our jobs, our relationships, our finances, our purpose, our roles and responsibilities as well as our contribution to the world around us.

Sometimes God will destroy that comfort to encourage us to step into our calling.

This can seem harsh, unfair and unjust.

But it's often that little push you need to obey your hearts desires and start to pursue your purpose and true calling.

For me, pursuing my purpose outworked itself in starting an Instagram account called @achievetheimpossible.

Today, I have the blessing and honour to have a platform that inspires and encourages millions of people around the world every single week to achieve their own impossible and pursue their calling.

Don't get caught up in comfort.

Your world needs you to pursue your purpose and chase your calling.

Be grateful in the seasons of discomfort. God is using them to stretch and grow your capacity to be able to become the person your dreams need you to be.

Time to refuel with passion and take that next step towards your impossible dream.

ACHIEVETHEIMPOSSIBLE

REFUEL WITH PASSION

When you feel like stopping, think about why you started.

I'm sure many of you have heard the above quote before...'When you feel like stopping, think about why you started' or something along those lines.

We've talked about taking that first step and starting the journey towards your impossible dream.

Today, I wanna talk about the moments along your journey when you experience something on the road that makes you question whether or not you continue on your journey.

Maybe you've come face to face with a road block, a situation that is out of your control that has plonked itself in the middle of your path.

Maybe you feel like you're running out of fuel and don't have the mental or physical capacity or strength to continue.

There's a thousand other reasons where you could be tempted to throw in the towel and quit on the journey.

If you're facing something like this in your life now, you'll know exactly what I'm talking about...there'll be a clear picture in your mind featuring this situation and decision.

Let's work through this step by step.

First, before we discuss re-connecting with your why, I want to you to answer a question for me.

Is this road ahead a true representation of your impossible dream? Is it a reflection of your heart's true purpose and desire?

If yes, fantastic! You're on the right track...

If your road isn't something you're truly passionate about, maybe this roadblock or time of challenge and difficulty is an opportunity to re-consider your journey and take the nearest exit so you can discover the road that may be the best path for you!

For those of you who know they are on the right road, but times and circumstances are difficult, making an unplanned detour is a very tempting prospect.

As the quote says, 'think about your why'.

Now I'm not going to give you a 12 point Path to Success here, we're going to focus on one thing at a time!

The sole thing I want you to consider when you're thinking of quitting, stopping or giving up is to re-connect with your why.

I want you to focus not on where you are but where you started this journey.

This start line could be 3 weeks, 3 months, 3 years or even 3 decades ago!

Go back to that place in your mind.

When @achievetheimpossible was 3 months old, we had a community of just over 3,000 followers. I had genuinely loved the first three months of the journey to my dreams of inspiring people.

Then I faced something on my journey...it wasn't a roadblock or an obstacle flying out of nowhere to stop me dead in my tracks, it was a little 'E' sitting at the very bottom of my emotional fuel gauge.

I was running on empty.

I became so caught up in the practicalities of creating content four times a day, manually going out and connecting with potential followers that I lost sight of my WHY, the very reason I began on this road in the first place.

Why did I start @achievetheimpossible?

To inspire, challenge and equip people to achieve their impossible dreams. I needed to re-connect with my WHY to tap into my initial passion and purpose that fuelled this journey for those first three months.

As you could imagine, I'm glad I re-connected with my why and re-fuelled with passion and purpose for the journey that followed.

As I write this, almost six years later, that same passion still fuels me on my journey today.

Think about your why. Then go deeper. Re-connect with it. Become immersed in it.

You started the journey for a reason.

Time to refuel with passion and take that next step towards your impossible dream.

FAITH

Prepare yourself for what you're praying for.

Make sure you stay ready so when it's your time, you're not try-ing to get ready.

ACHIEVETHEIMPOSSIBLE

PREPARE = PRE-PRAYER

Prepare yourself for what you're praying for. Make sure you stay ready so when it's your time, you're not trying to get ready.

Have you ever found yourself wishing, hoping and praying for something you desperately desire and then find yourself wondering why it's not happening the way you thought it should?

I know I have.

It's too easy to throw a line out like 'I'm praying for this to happen' or one that's possibly even more common, 'my prayers are with you'.

Having these wishes, hopes and prayers are all good things to speak over your own life and the lives of those around you.

But they shouldn't end with words.

Your prayers are just the start.

This is when reality hits.

It's not enough to merely speak something into being and sit back hoping that all your wants and desires be brought to you on a silver platter.

We need to couple these prayers with action.

Daily, consistent, intentional action that prepares us for our prayers to manifest themselves.

Praying to be become a millionaire?

How are you treating, managing and respecting the money you have now?

Praying for a new car?

How are you treating the car you've got now? Is it clean, tidy and loved?

Praying for that promotion at work?

How are you respecting the position you're in right now? Are you going the extra mile, doing over and above what is expected in your current role?

Praying for better relationships?

Now here's a real wake up call! Look in the mirror...How are you treating you? How are you respecting and valuing the relationship you have with yourself and your life?

Praying to compete in the Tokyo 2020 Olympics?

What are you doing today to get you closer to that milestone? Are you challenging your physical capacity, as well as developing a world class mindset?

Prepare for your prayers.

Speak your future into being by doing what you can with what you have in this very moment.

It's all connected.
Your gifts,
your purpose,
your circumstances,
your imperfections.

It's your journey and
your destiny.

It's moulding you.

Embrace it.

ACHIEVETHEIMPOSSIBLE

YOUR GOD-GIVEN OPPORTUNITY

I truly believe God never gives you a dream without the talents, skills, abilities and characteristics to achieve it.

Does this mean you'll sail through life accomplishing everything because it's brought to you on a silver platter?

Not at all. It's probably going to be the complete opposite to be honest.

What it does mean, however, is that you now have an 11–letter word that has been given to you...

'O P P O R T U N I T Y'

You have the opportunity right now to live life in the direction of your dreams.

The opportunity to develop your skills, talents and abilities to be able to get you to a place where you can accomplish the dreams and desires of your heart.

That opportunity comes in the form of a seed. A seed that God has planted.

Now it's your turn to give that seed the best conditions to grow, through the best soil, constant watering and access to sunlight.

I'll give you some creative license here...you choose what the elements of soil, water and sunlight personally mean for you and your life, but for me they would be as follows...

Environment - surrounding myself with people and ideas that inspire, support and uplift me.

Refreshment - hydrating myself with things that lead to my personal development. Books, podcasts, speeches, sermons, etc.

Inspiration - allowing myself to be present and enjoy the moment. Spending time with God and his creation to bring light and love into my life.

Everything you need to achieve your impossible is within you.

God's planted the seed. Now it's up to you to create that healthy environment, water it and give it sunlight!

There will be a way.

ACHIEVETHEIMPOSSIBLE

HOPE IN THE UNKNOWN

There will be a way.

Imagine you're about to go through one of those big bushy-hedge mazes in those adventure parks. (I've never actually done this, but do remember seeing it on an episode of Modern Family, so I'm assuming they're real!)

You are just about to take your first step into the unknown.

You're a little nervous, but excited for the journey ahead.

There is a thought that gives you a glimmer of hope as you enter this bushy human puzzle... 'there will be a way'.

As you get further into the thick of the maze, you are very likely going to get stressed out, lose your bearings, doubt yourself and find yourself completely and utterly lost.

But you don't throw in the towel, sit down and give up. Why? Because even in the midst of chaos and confusion, you know one thing to be true; there will be a way.

When we know there is a way out of our current situation, we have hope for the future.

Do we need to know every single step of the journey? Absolutely not.

Will we know what the path looks like? Again, not at all.

Have we even seen what the exit looks like?!

These questions could very easily turn into paralyzing fears and doubts unless we focus on that one truth... 'there will be a way'.

You may not be in the middle of a maze made of hedges that you'd seen on a TV show, but you may be in a situation right now in your life that doesn't have a clear exit path.

You may feel stuck in a job, a season, a relationship or a mindset that you're doing your best to navigate. You may have been encountering dead end after dead end after dead end.

You could even be wondering if this is it. Is this where I'm going spend the rest of my life?

If you're feeling like you don't know how to keep going, I've got five words that could change your life...

'There will be a way.'

With faith in knowing there is a way out of your situation, you can continue with your head held high confident that there is light at the end of the maze (ok, tunnel...just wanted to keep with the metaphor!)

You may not be able to see the end right now...there may be twists, turns and corners ahead in your journey.

But there will be a way.

No matter how dark, how lost or how hopeless your situation seems, know this truth; there will be a way.

Here's an interesting thought...

Today's quote doesn't say 'there will be an end'.

It says 'there will be a WAY'. Do you know what that tells me?

The journey, also known as the way is more important than the end result or destination.

Who we become, how we develop, what we pick up along the journey are the keys we require to reach our destination.

Sometimes the destination won't reveal itself until we've picked up, learned, developed, strengthened and discovered things about ourselves that we will require for our eventual next maze.

If you're in a situation that's surrounded by confusion and a sense of the unknown, take hope in these five words...there will be a way.

Keep your head up, keep your faith and keep walking step by step until you discover that way.

There will be a way.

Faith says no matter what lays ahead...

I believe I have been given the gifts, talents and abilities to bring my dreams to reality.

Even when I don't see the exact details of the HOW.

ACHIEVETHEIMPOSSIBLE

FEAR AND FAITH

Live a fearless life.

On the journey to your impossible dream, there will be times when you are faced with an unknown challenge or obstacle.

This will force you to take a stance and choose the mindset you walk into the unknown with.

When we don't know the details and exact steps of the upcoming path, our thoughts have a major influence on our journey.

We have one of two choices...

1. FEAR

Fear is powerful. Fear is very commonly the default setting for an unknown challenge ahead. Fear focuses on the negative possibilities of the unknown and can infect our thinking to a point of paralysis.

How many times has fear stopped you from stepping into the unknown?

I know for myself personally, fear has kept me from pursuing something I knew deep down had my name on it.

Fear can restrict our mindset and paralyse our actions heading into the unknown.

Fear can cause us to question the path ahead and sow the seeds of doubt in our mind.

Fear can consume our thinking and dictate our future.

BUT...I have good news!

There is another option...

2. FAITH

Faith says no matter what lays ahead, I believe I am capable of living out the journey set out ahead of me.

Faith says this journey I'm on has its purpose in my life.

Faith says that no matter what lays ahead, I trust each step I take is the right step in the direction of my destiny.

Faith is something we cultivate and develop in our lives by connecting ourselves to our WHY.

Faith is built by acknowledging and respecting our true passion and purpose, and allowing those truths to direct our path.

Faith says no matter what lays ahead, I have been given the belief, gifts, talents and abilities to bring my dreams to reality, even when I don't see the exact details of the HOW.

My recommendation...choose faith. Faith is the light that drives out the darkness of fear. Be fearless and develop faith for what sets your soul on fire.

Sight is what we see with our eyes.

Vision is what we see with our hearts.

ACHIEVETHEIMPOSSIBLE

VISION OVER SIGHT

Imagine with me a beautiful house atop the cliffs overlooking the powerful ocean.

You treasure the moments when the sun is shining, the crisp, cool summer breeze rolls in through the sheer curtains and life is wonderful.

Suddenly, the weather turns and a storm comes rolling in. You close the windows and doors and watch as the wind transforms the calm sea into a wild ocean.

You wouldn't have a beautiful beachfront house and demolish it when the seas are rough and the weather turns.

Yes, the view out your window might not be perfect. Remember this...when circumstances outside change, your foundations within don't.

If you truly believe in your heart you are where you're meant to be right now, stand strong.

There will be strong winds, rough seas that, at times, will threaten you and you can guarantee negative thoughts will try and eat away at your self-belief.

Stand strong.

Reinforce those foundations.

Become so focused on your passion, your purpose and your mission that you can see beyond the current storm you're surrounded by.

To see beyond the storm, you've got to look up and focus your vision.

Stop looking at the damp, soggy ground beneath you or the wind battering your beliefs.

Look to the future.
Look to the possibilities of tomorrow.
Look beyond what you can currently see.

We're called to use our VISION not our SIGHT.

*"The only thing worse than being blind is having
sight but no vision." -Helen Keller*

Sight is what we see with our eyes.

The bills, the obstacles, the mistakes we've made, the people we've hurt, the ones who've hurt us.

Vision is what we see with our hearts.

The opportunities, the potential, the upcoming breakthrough, the hope, the untapped capacity, achieving what seems impossible.

Let's choose vision over sight.

Sight happens by default. Vision happens on purpose.

Sometimes we have to experience things we don't understand just so God can bring us to a place He needs us to be.

Never doubt the season He has you in.

ACHIEVETHEIMPOSSIBLE

YOUR BEST IS YET TO COME

Hindsight is a beautiful thing!

We've all been through seasons and stages of our lives where we don't feel in control at all.

We can't understand why things are happening the way they are and definitely don't understand why they are happening to us!

> *Sometimes God will take us through a season of*
> *confusion to position us where we need to be.*

It could be the recent relationship that has broken your heart, it could be from out of nowhere your boss told you that your company was downsizing and you no longer have a job.

It could be moving to an entirely different suburb, city or even country that brings this season of confusion that challenges your positive mindset.

No matter what season of confusion you're going through, everything will make sense in due time. Hindsight is a beautiful thing!

Do me a quick favour; look back 3 years, 5 years or 20 years back to the time of your first serious relationship break-up.

It hurt like hell then but would you say you're in a better place now?

I have a feeling 99% of you would be thanking your lucky stars every morning your prayers about him or her being 'the one' weren't answered!

Look back at the last time you packed up and moved cities.

Those first few months where you knew no one and needed a GPS just to tell you how to get to the supermarket for milk and bread seemed like they'd never end!

It's too easy to forget these moments of uncertainty and confusion that have been dotted along our life's journey. Not only are they there to grow, develop and strengthen us, they reinforce how important faith in the unseen truly is.

Next time you're in a season that doesn't make sense, just remember...you're viewing things from the present moment you're in.

Despite your best efforts, your perception and perspective is limited when you're looking at your own situation, especially whilst being in the middle of your own situation!

Even though we can't see the future, God can.

This season is positioning you exactly where you need to be for your next season in life.

Have faith during the confusion.
Trust everything will work out just as it needs to.
You've got this and God's got you.
Your best is yet to come.

Faith often finds its voice in your darkest times.

It's that light at the end of the tunnel that whispers...

'Everything's going to be okay, you've got this'.

ACHIEVETHEIMPOSSIBLE

FAITH OVER FEAR

Faith and fear both demand you believe in something you cannot see. You choose!

Faith or fear...which one will you feed?

Within us live two opposing and competing powers. These powers are sitting dormant until we are presented with a thought or a feeling that we need to seek assurance for.

Maybe it's a thought of the future...
Where will you be?
What will you be doing?
Who will you surround yourself with?

These thoughts require you to dig deeper; it's almost like getting a second opinion...do I fear the unknown or do I have faith when presented with these questions?

Fear loves to put its sneaky little hand up even when you don't ask for its opinion. Fear loves to step in by default when thoughts of the future come up. Fear will always jump to the front, unless you choose to feed your faith!

The secret is simple. Feed your faith and develop a consistent relationship with it. Faith is that quiet assurance. It's not the loud, overwhelming, attention seeking voice like fear is.

Faith often finds its voice in your darkest times; it's that light at the end of the tunnel that whispers 'everything's gonna be okay, you've got this'.

Here's the cool thing about faith; it's naturally quiet and can often go unnoticed, but when you call on it, it becomes one of strongest forces known to man.

Next time you're presented with the choice to feed your fear or your faith, make that intentional decision to put your trust in faith.

- Know who you are
- Acknowledge your true potential
- Find positive statements that inspire you (Bible verses, affirmations, mantras, quotes etc.), write them down and say them over and over.

Your self-talk is the key to building your faith.

Next time uncertainty pops up, choose faith! Your best is yet to come.

Live as though your prayers have already been answered.

ACHIEVETHEIMPOSSIBLE

ANSWERED PRAYERS

Live as though your prayers have already been answered.

What are your dreams, your prayers, your ambitions for today and the future?

Do me a favour and think about the person in the world right now who is reflecting the life of your dreams.

Is it Serena Williams, Richard Branson, Elon Musk or Ariana Grande? Maybe it's someone in your circle who you admire for who they are and what they do.

Here's my key strategy; live like the person you want to become.

If you want to be a body-builder, start living like a body-builder, start eating what a body-builder eats and dedicate the same amount of time in the gym as they do.

Maybe you want to be an Olympic Swimmer? Study someone who inspires you and start trying to match their routine. How many hours are they in the pool? What are they eating? Who do they surround themselves with? Maybe you want to be the next Mark Zuckerberg or Kylie Jenner? Study their lives, see how they started, then start living with that in mind!

It's time to start living each and every single day with your future in mind!

Your dreams aren't going to come true by themselves. It's up to you to bring them into reality!

The good news is you've got everything inside you to make those dreams come true. Now is the time to start living like you truly believe you deserve it.

The moment we align ourselves to our dreams of the future in the moment we are in now, is the moment those dreams begin to flesh themselves out in our life.

Stop stressing about the future and start working on the present.

ACHIEVETHEIMPOSSIBLE

IT'S ALL WORKED OUT

God has already worked out the thing that has been stressing you out.

I don't know about you, but for me, when stress sneaks in, it's often when I'm trying to figure out the exact details of a future event.

Whether it's a Keynote to a group of people, a conversation to clear something up with a friend or an upcoming event or product launch...stress loves to pop its head up when there's something looming in the near future.

I would often catch myself dancing with stress and would immerse myself in stressful thinking of the practicalities of the near future.

This thinking soon escalates to analyzing. It starts to grow and grow and eventually ends up feeding off itself and turning into over-thinking and birthing anxious thoughts.

This was until I realized something that changed the way I thought...we get so caught up thinking about and stressing over the future because we can't control it.

As the future is always one step away from us, we are never going to have total control over it.

Negative thinking will get you to over-think the future, what you can't control, and distract you from the present, what you can control.

Stop stressing about the future and start working on the present.

The future is God's domain. The present is ours.

Stop trying to supervise God and trust that He has the future sorted out.

The moment you put your trust and faith in His sovereignty in the future becomes the very moment you can let go of what's coming and focus on what's here.

You do you what you can do.
God's got the future laid out before you.

Free yourself from trying to control what God is doing and start focusing on what you can control, your next step.

God has already worked out the thing that has been stressing you out.

You're not going to have everything you need from the start.

Your provisions are waiting for you as you take the steps towards your impossible dream.

ACHIEVETHEIMPOSSIBLE

PROVISION ON THE JOURNEY

You and I don't have the time, finances, strategies, people, skills or resources to bring our impossible dream to life.

Simple as that. Sorry to burst your bubble, but we just don't.

I know for myself personally...I don't have the exact strategy, plans, vision, people, finances or resources to achieve my impossible dream.

I found myself focusing on what I lacked and what I still needed to collect before embarking on the journey ahead. I took it up with God for clarity, wisdom and a bit of divine direction.

'God, I don't have everything I need for the journey ahead...as soon as I've got those things, we can start!'

The answer I heard from God instantly changed my perception of the journey ahead.

He said 'you're not going to have everything you need all the time. I will provide your provisions as you take the steps towards the journey ahead.'

As you make progress towards your impossible dream, God will give you what you need when the time comes.

Trust and have faith in His provision along your journey.

If we had everything we thought we needed now, we wouldn't need to trust or have faith in the path ahead. We would do it with our limited knowledge, skills, wisdom and experience.

The provision...the finances, people, skills, time, energy and resources are on the journey ahead waiting for you.

You're going to have to trust in those steps and start the journey with faith.

Trust and faith from the first step ensures we aren't doing this walk in our own limited strength and wisdom. I want to be someone who trusts in God's plans for my life; they are far greater than I could ever think or imagine.

The provision will meet you as you take those steps to your impossible dream.

Trust and have faith in your next steps. Ask God and He will guide you in the right direction towards what you need next.

The decisions we make in the day to day compound to influence our entire life.

ACHIEVETHEIMPOSSIBLE

GOD'S POINT OF VIEW

Just like you, I've heard a million different definitions of popular life-defining words like success, patience, trust and wisdom but this one here is one of the best I have ever heard.

"Wisdom is seeing life from God's point of view. Wisdom is the ability to make decisions the way God makes decisions." - Rick Warren

In our day-to-day lives we make decisions either consciously or subconsciously every moment we breathe.

Some of these decisions are small and insignificant for what they are, while others are large and have a direct influence on our lives.

The decisions we make in the day to day compound to influence our entire life.

This is why we need to tap into wisdom to make decisions that are not just based on our emotions and feelings in the moment but are the best choices in terms of our perspective and long-term progress towards our destination.

When I need to make a key decision about a big choice or change of direction, I will always try and remove my emotions and feelings from it and change my perspective.

I like to see it, just as Rick Warren said in the quote, from 'God's point of you.'

I think that's I really cool way to put it.

When we see things from God's point of view, we can see not just the step we're on right now but we also get a much clearer picture of the steps that we have travelled on in the past and the direction we are heading with our next steps.

When we use wisdom to guide these steps, we are making the decision that is best for our future based on the lessons of the past and acknowledging the present situation we are in this very moment.

Today, let's grow in wisdom and live a life making decisions from God's point of view.

Take one step forward.

Step forward with confidence in the face of the unknown.

Step forward with faith when you can't see the path ahead.

Step forward with boldness when others are hesitant.

Take one step forward.

ACHIEVETHEIMPOSSIBLE

ONE STEP FORWARD

Keep moving forward. One day you'll look back and say with confidence, 'Now I know why I had to keep going'.

Take one step forward.

Step forward with confidence in the face of the unknown.

Step forward with faith when you can't see the path ahead.

Step forward with boldness when others are hesitant.

Take one step forward.

You may be facing a mountain. Take one step forward.

You may have just conquered a mountain. Take one step forward.

Our decision to prioritize progress shouldn't be based on circumstances, but on consistency.

No one has climbed a mountain in one step. But every mountain has been conquered one step at a time.

Some of our next steps are scary, with the fear of the unknown staring us square in the face.

Is the next step in the right direction?

Is the foundation stable?

What's ahead past that step?

Is this step for me?

I can tell you one thing in absolute confidence...the answers to these questions will reveal themselves as you take that step.

Whether you have recently conquered your mountain or are approaching your next challenge, the answers to the unknown are in that next step.

Until we take that step, fear will be the default feeling. Fear of the unknown, fear of failure, fear of other people's opinions.

Fear develops when we are stagnant.

Fear comes along when we are about to approach our next step.

That's a good thing.

Fear is our greatest push to what's next.

Use that fear to help propel you to your next step.

Maybe it's walking though the front door of that gym.

Maybe it's registering a business name.

Maybe it's delivering a resumé.

Maybe it's asking that girl on your heart out on a date.

Maybe it's saying yes to that date.

There is power in that next step.

When you reach that next step, you will have access to everything you need for the steps after that.

Your only responsibility is that step. The step towards your purpose, your passion and your calling.

Despite the fear of the unknown, build your faith, trust and hope and with confidence and boldness and take one step forward.

FEAR

Don't let fear be your brake or steering wheel.

You are in control of direction and momentum.

Use fear to fuel you.

ACHIEVETHEIMPOSSIBLE

USE FEAR AS FUEL

Don't fear failure. Fear being in the exact same place next year as you are today.

We've talked about God's point of view and looking back on your life from the perspective of the future and using that perspective to fuel your decisions for today.

Now I want to share a little more on the fear that can hold us back from stepping into all we are called to be.

Let's talk about harnessing that fear and using it to fuel that next step.

First, a question to kick start our thinking;

'Where will you be in 12 months from now?'

What was the first thought that crossed through your mind?

Was it a meticulous plan of the exact person you want to be, the detailed figures you're wanting to make and the specific achievement you'd like beside your name?

Or, if we can be real for just a moment, was the first thought that crossed through your mind...'Ahhh, crap! A year from now...hmmm. I don't exactly know, but I guess I'd like to do...xxx'.

Now I'm gonna take a wild stab here and say that the last answer I shared would represent many of the responses.

How am I so certain?

Because to be completely honest with you, that above response is my own personal response.

I don't know exactly where I will be in 365 days from today. I'm not sure what I will be doing, how I will be doing it, or who I'll be doing it with.

Let's look back to last year, exactly 365 days ago...for one, I had no idea things like the Achieve the Impossible App would even be a thing, I would never have picked that a couple of days ago, I would have done my first international Keynote and I definitely wouldn't have been able to exactly see the people I'm blessed enough to be doing life with today.

Regardless of whether or not we have a clear vision for 365 days from now just yet, there is one thing I know for certain.

Our focus must be on the steps we are taking each and every single day.

If you don't have a clear vision of your life 12 months from now, focus on creating a clear vision for today. Then a clear vision for tomorrow.

Begin stepping in the direction of that vision, and as you progress, the path ahead will reveal itself clearer and clearer to you.

You have a tremendous amount of untapped potential and opportunities within these next 12 months.

Where there is great opportunity, there will naturally be an element of fear. That fear can either be the accelerator that moves things forward, the steering wheel that guides our path, or the brake that brings our lives to a complete stop.

There will always be an element of fear when we approach greatness...the secret is to harness that energy into propelling you towards your dreams.

Don't let fear be your brake or steering wheel. You are in control of direction and momentum. Use fear to fuel you, because your next 12 months start...right now!

God will show when it's time to know.

ACHIEVETHEIMPOSSIBLE

FEAR OR FAITH

99% of the things you're worrying about never happen.

When you're in a season of unknown, a season of confusion, a season of lack or a season where things just aren't making sense, I want you to know something, a little sentence that has the power to release the fear of the unknown...

'God will show when it's time to know.'

This is a concept I'm just beginning to wrap my head around because it ironically goes against everything I once thought to true.

What's my next step?

Where's the next opportunity?

How can I do this?

Is this even for me?

I want the answers! I love knowing where I'm going and what I can expect to encounter along the way on this journey called life.

If we knew the answers, we would be able to map out our life plan to the finest detail and ensure we're progressing in the right direction with every step we take.

We would save time, eliminate heartache, minimize failure and protect our resources.

There's a reason we don't have access to the future and its mysteries.

I think that if we knew what was to come in the future, we would risk losing the precious moment of the present.

When we think of the future, we are faced with two choices. We can either trust and have faith in what is to come or we can worry and allow fear to access our hearts and minds.

Here's the thing, both faith and fear of the future require us to believe in something we cannot see.

I truly believe that when we need to access a glimpse of our future, we see it through our God-given dreams, desires, goals and ambition.

Have heart knowing that if you can't see it, it's not for your eyes yet.

Let's appreciate the moment we're in right now. That's what we have been given access to and direct control over. Once we own this, we look to the unknown future full of faith and trust.

I'm learning to be grateful for the unknown.

It allows me to focus on the known.

RISK

Your comfort must give way to your calling.

Your present must give way to your potential.

ACHIEVETHEIMPOSSIBLE

YOU ARE CAPABLE

"Deep down, you know exactly what you are capable of. There's even moments where you get a glimpse of all the potential you have. You can get there. You just have to be willing to sacrifice the habits, things and situations that are standing in the way of your success." - Idil Ahmed

As I was writing this book, I was inspired to write something that I have battled with my entire life; my relationship with risk. The next few chapters on risk have the power to unlock mindsets and belief systems that have been holding you back from your true potential.

Before we do something crazy and run to risk, let's take stock of where we are today and the foundational beliefs in our potential and true capacity.

In the day-to-day act of living, waking up, coffee, breakfast, school drop-offs, work, more coffee, home, homework, dinner, finish off emails, glass or two of (insert fav drink here), collapse on couch, Netflix etc. we can become disconnected with our true potential and capacity.

You are being pulled from all sides; your family, your boss, your colleagues, your partner, your friends and even your dog.

You can be forgiven for prioritizing the present over the future.

To set up these chapters on healthy and personal-capacity fuelled risk, I want you to invest a moment or two searching deep within yourself.

> *What's on your heart for this year?*
> *What is one thing you would look back on come 31st December and be proud*
> *of your personal accomplishment?*
> *What's something that scares you?*

This is the very thing we're going to focus on in this section on risk.

We're focusing on it because with every achievement that challenges our personal capacity and unlocks our potential, there will be an element of risk.

Risk is scary. Risk stares you in the face from afar and says don't you dare approach. Don't even try.

This is when you're faced with a decision to make, and the best (and also worst!) thing about it is you're the only one who can make it!

As you make this decision to run to risk, the regret of not running has to be stronger than your personal comfort.

> *Your comfort must give way to your calling.*
> *Your present must give way to your potential.*

Think about the one thing on your heart, the thing that helps you step into your calling and potential. The thing with risk looming all over it.

That's the risk we're running towards in the next few chapters. Let's build the strength, self-belief, courage, boldness and tenacity to run to risk.

Now is always the right time to do that thing that's on your heart.

ACHIEVETHEIMPOSSIBLE

NOW IS THE PERFECT TIME

You can't always wait for the perfect time. Sometimes, you have to dare to do it because life is too short to wonder what might have been.

We laid the foundation of this section on risk by identifying the one thing we want to accomplish this year that challenges our potential and capacity. Naturally this will always have an element of risk associated with it.

We're not running to risk for a laugh and a good time, we're running to risk because that dream in our hearts for this year is worth pursuing!

When faced with the potential of risk, we often come up with thoughts and reasons to justify our lack of momentum or progress.

'I don't know how!'
'I don't have the money!'
'I don't have the connections!'

But one of the most common excuses I hear (I know, because I hear it from myself) is a little sentence that has killed more dreams and crushed more souls than most...

'It's not the right time.'

It's one of the most powerful excuses because it bulldozes every other excuse by default.

You'll always meet more people, money comes and goes, but once time is gone...it's gone forever.

This excuse becomes our default without us even realizing it.

I remember when I was wanting to launch an app, a podcast and a book (these are some of my risks as I am writing this in 2019). But they were also my goals for last year and the year before that.

Sadly, I put my insecurities ahead of my identity and my convenience over my calling.

Looking back now, each excuse I held was based on timing.

First, I told myself the Instagram algorithms were affecting posts, then someone else launched a podcast and gosh, I couldn't do that too!

Next, as I was dreaming of my App, another one came on the market. Nope, can't do that now. I better wait til the marketing heat dies down on that one.

The exact same situation with my book launch...it just wasn't quite the right time.

Here's what I learnt; there's never a right time to do the thing that's on your heart.

The right time will never simply show up...you've got the time, now it's up to you to make it right!

Looking back, I've felt the pain of regret and don't want to let the fear of risk lead to regret again.

Now is the time to look risk dead square in the eyes and say 'ready or not, here I come'.

Today, we start.

ACHIEVETHEIMPOSSIBLE

START SOMETHING NEW

Never be afraid to try something new, because life gets boring when you stay within the limits of what you already know.

We've just told risk we're coming for it.

We've made the decision to put our calling over our comfort and choose to be led by faith not fear.

Now it's the time to start.

We're starting right now because we have been given the time, and we've got complete power and control to make it the 'right time'.

We've made the decision to go after that thing that's on our heart, the thing we've always wanted to do, the thing that has been too risky.

Not anymore.

Today, we start.

There is huge power in the start. When we start, we have the luxury of being on home ground.

We are making more decisions for ourselves, rather than having to make decisions based on responses which we will have to inevitably do down the road.

Today, we start.

We're filled fresh with enthusiasm, passion and driven by our desire to accomplish something meaningful this year.

Yesterday, we may have had a loss to our name, we may have stumbled and fallen...but we've picked ourselves up.

Today, we start.

We look to the future with our heads held high, the hopes of a brighter future with that dream in our heart knowing that we are valiantly pursuing it despite the risk.

We know our dream, we know we are capable of achieving it, we know we've got the time and today, we start.

We start the journey as we run to risk.

Mistakes aren't meant to stop us, they are there to direct us.

ACHIEVETHEIMPOSSIBLE

LOSE THE FEAR OF BEING WRONG

"To live a creative life, we must lose our fear of being wrong." - Joseph Chilton Pearce

We've started on our journey running towards risk!

Our dreams are alive and more real than ever. We're thinking, planning, trusting and breathing life into our potential.

As I'm writing this, I'm organizing the final details of the Achieve the Impossible Podcast launch and am planning out the finer details of the very book you're holding.

Together, we're running towards risk!

One of the first obstacles we're going to face on this journey towards risk is one that often strikes a damaging blow to our pride and can sometimes take us to our knees.

As you embark on this journey, I can almost guarantee that we will take a wrong turn from time to time, we will read the map wrong (I'll take the hit, I'm the navigator, sorry!) which will send us off course.

When you've taken a wrong turn driving, what is your first thought? DAMN IT. (Yep, me too!)

What's your second thought?

Is it 'Ahh, I've stuffed up. I'm gonna just pull over and sit here until either the roads and maps magically change in my favor or someone comes to rescue me?'

Or do we think, 'Ok, what's the quickest way to get back on my path?'

When we stuff up, make a mistake, choose the wrong software, tell the wrong people or say the wrong thing, we don't just pack up our dreams and hide. NO.

We pick ourselves back up. We face what we believe to be the right direction and we MOVE FORWARD.

I don't care if you start by walking...one timid step at a time, just start!

Those small steps gain momentum and eventually lead to a jog, then before you know it, you're back running!

Anytime you embark on an unknown journey you're going to make mistakes.

Mistakes aren't meant to stop us, they are there to direct us.

How you respond is the only thing I want you to focus on. Respond with reflection, movement and momentum in the direction of your dreams.

On our journey, we're going to make mistakes and take wrong turns from time to time, but we choose to pick ourselves back up and get back on that journey!

We're not staying stuck, we're running to risk!

The risk we perceive in our own mind is often actually far greater than it truly is in reality.

ACHIEVETHEIMPOSSIBLE

INVEST IN RISK

"Inaction breeds doubt and fear. Action breeds confidence and courage. If you want to conquer fear, do not sit at home and think about it. Go out and get busy." - Dale Carnegie

Sounds like I'm about to write a chapter on Warren Buffet's worst nightmare.

But that's not the risk I'm talking about and it's not the investing I'm talking about. (Sleep tight, Warren.)

This risk I'm talking about is the thing that stands between you and your 'impossible' dream.

The dream that you've told yourself is too strong, too powerful and too insurmountable to climb.

The risk we perceive in our own minds is often actually far greater than it truly is in reality.

I remember as a child visiting a museum and being fascinated by a scary looking dinosaur down the other side of the room.

It looked ferocious and intimidating from across the room, and as I walked closer and closer, the dinosaur, through the magic of perspective, got bigger and bigger.

That's where I feel we are at right now on our journey towards risk. We've identified the risk standing between us and our dreams, and we're taking the tentative first steps towards it.

As we step closer and closer to risk, it will look bigger. You'll start to compare the size of it to you, and don't be surprised if it grows each step you take.

But, have faith...

The closer I got to the dinosaur, the bigger it became.

I had a choice. Do I let fear determine my next steps? Or do I have faith in those next steps?

I continued walking step by step towards the prehistoric creature. Then something strange happened...

Yes, the closer I got to the creature, the bigger it became. But then something else came into the picture.

The closer I got, the more detail I was noticing.

What I thought were once bone-crunching teeth were merely a synthetic matte white plastic and what I once thought was impenetrable leather-like skin was just flaking, old, crusty paint.

Those eyes that glared at me from across the room were now nothing but big marble sized spheres of glass.

When we step towards fear, yes it gets bigger.

But as we invest in faith and continue to live our lives in the direction of our dreams, we expose the master of risk...FEAR.

False

Evidence°

Appearing

Real

Invest in those extra steps this week...as you get closer to risk, you'll be positioned to point out the finer details.

You're soon going to realize it's not as scary as it once seemed.

GROWTH

Growth always involves pruning.

ACHIEVETHEIMPOSSIBLE

PURPOSE TO THE PRUNING

Remember that growth always involves some pruning.

Recently, while on a holiday with friends in Tuscany, we toured some stunning wineries.

One thing that caught my attention was a comment a certain vinedresser mentioned. It was relating to the severe pruning these vines get after the harvesting season.

"At the end of each harvest, we must prune down the vines. The vines grow all season and bear fruit, but then we must prune the old stuff away by cutting off most of the vine that extends outwards. This allows the vine to rest and prepare for its next season of fruit."

This comment really stood out to me and got me thinking.

We've got to prune the things in our lives that are no longer growing. They've served their purpose, they've done what they were meant to do, and now it's time to prepare for the next season.

The reason for the extensive pruning these vines go through is so the plant can rest and recuperate after a season of exerting all of it's energy producing the harvest.

It needs to take a break, re-prioritize and prepare for the season ahead.

Without this extent of pruning, the plant would not be able to bear that level of fruit again, because its energy is depleted supporting the vines that have already produced their fruit and served their purpose.

How strongly does this relate to our everyday lives?

We need to prune back the non-producing vines in our lives in order to prioritize our energy and prepare for our next season of growth!

Your first step doesn't
have to be perfect,
polished or precise.

It just has to be in the
right direction.

ACHIEVETHEIMPOSSIBLE

YOUR FIRST STEP

Just for a moment, let's look ahead at the remainder of your life here on earth. Every person you're going to meet, every decision you're going to make, every project you're going to accomplish and every dream you're going to achieve.

Chances are your mind may be going into overdrive with the possibilities of the future right now!

It's a sometimes very daunting vision to try and visualize from the perspective and position you're at right now in this very moment.

We're gonna get real and discuss some practical strategies today!

First, let's hone in on a particular part of the big-picture vision and focus on one specific, individual project.

Maybe it's the book you're desperate to start writing with the goal of publishing it for the world to read.

Maybe it's a podcast idea that's been simmering on the back-burners and now is the time to fire up the launch.

Maybe it's the business idea that seems completely out of your depth or comfort zone, but you know can make a huge difference to your family.

Or maybe it's finding a new job, a new title or a new career...where you work now just isn't bringing the best out of you and you feel you are ready to enter a new season.

No matter the details of the next season you're stepping into, there is one thing they all have in common.

They ALL require ONE STEP.

"A journey of a thousand miles begins with a single step." - *Lao Tzu*

You and I both know it's often the first step that is the hardest.

This first step is the one that identifies direction, initiates progression and facilitates momentum.

I want to take a moment to speak into your first step.

This first step doesn't need to be a leap, and it definitely doesn't need to be meticulously rehearsed or perfect.

The only factor we should be considering when we are evaluating the progress of this first step is one of my favourite words, 'direction'.

I don't care if this first step is almost invisible to the naked eye. In fact, often this first step is a necessary change in mindset or self-belief, and can't be seen immediately.

As long as you're stepping in the direction of your dreams, the apparent measure of distance is irrelevant.

A 300-yard drive off the tee in a game of golf has the exact same numeric value as a 2-foot putt to sink the ball in the hole.

Take your first step today in the direction of your dreams.

Even if you haven't perfected it and don't have all the answers. Because once you're ready to take step two, you've already clocked up experience on your step counter.

Do the best you can with what's in your hands right now.

The step doesn't have to be polished, perfect or precise. It just has to be in the right direction.

No matter what journey you're about to embark on, take that first step. This step can begin the journey of a thousand miles.

BE willing and BECOME able.

ACHIEVETHEIMPOSSIBLE

ARE YOU WILLING?

When I fly, I always try to get a seat in an exit row.

For any of my fellow exit row buddies who love the extra legroom out there, we know the one question we get asked before we get buckled in, "In the unlikely event of an emergency...(you know the rest)...are you WILLING and ABLE?"

We need to be both WILLING and ABLE to fulfil our role in the position we're in.

Life asks us a slightly different question...

'ARE YOU WILLING?'

The question is not if you're good enough, competent enough, capable enough or if you've got your life sorted.

The question is 'are you WILLING?'

Too often, we discredit ourselves because of our shortcomings. We know our areas of weakness better than most and know what we are working on.

This leads us to ask ourselves 'Am I able?' before we answer 'I am willing!'

Our willingness is the foundation we build our ability on.

You can have all the natural gifts, talents and abilities in the world, but if you're not willing, nobody can make you do something you won't do.

Let's flip to the other side of the story.

If you are willing, even when you're not completely able, God can use you to do crazy things (maybe even make those impossible dreams of yours come true).

The fear of failure is real. It's something I personally have to confront on a daily basis. But I would much rather be willing to fail at something, than not even try.

When you get to the end of your time on earth, could you look back and honestly say you were willing?

Saying yes to God's opportunities allows him access to build into your life those things you need to bring your dreams into reality.

BE willing and BECOME able.

Your focus determines your future.

ACHIEVETHEIMPOSSIBLE

DISAPPOINTMENT TO DESTINY

Sometimes our greatest disappointments lead us to our greatest blessings. Trust His plan even when you don't understand the path.

Our greatest disappointments can lead to our destiny!

This chapter is for anyone who has faced a disappointment recently or is going through a season of transition between planting the seeds and harvesting the fruit.

In order for us to achieve the impossible dreams that have been put on our hearts, we are going to have to grow.

As a caterpillar grows through its life cycle, our personal growth is going to demand we make changes to our lives.

Now this change hopefully doesn't involve a cocoon and slimy wings, but it will require a transitioning.

Change means in order to pick up something new, we will have to let go of what's already in our hands.

Letting go of what's known and familiar to you can seem like a major disappointment. Maybe you feel like you've dropped what was in your hands... maybe it's been ripped out of them.

No matter the circumstance, letting go of the old makes a way for the new. It could be a relationship, a home, a town, a job, a mindset or even an unhealthy expectation of yourself.

We have two choices when we lose what's in our hands;

> 1. *We can continue to look at what we've dropped and fill our hearts with disappointment.*
>
> 2. *We make the intentional decision to focus on what's new and actively seek after our next opportunity.*

Your focus determines your future.

Are you going to continue to look down in disappointment or choose to look up towards destiny?

Losing what's in your hands can be a humbling and very vulnerable season. But no season lasts forever; spring comes after the winter.

There's a good chance this season may be uncomfortable. That discomfort isn't there to hold us back and bury us...it is there to encourage us to focus on what's next.

When a mother eagle is teaching her eaglets to fly, she slowly starts to remove the soft cushioning of feathers and hair from the nest.

The foundation of sticks and thorns begin to cause discomfort for the small birds and they quickly learn to leave the nest and fly.

Eagles know discomfort leads to opportunity, so choose to focus on what's next.

It's time for you to confront your discomfort and turn your disappointment into destiny.

Leave the nest, you're ready to fly!

TIME

Create space in your day to follow through on your habit. Be disciplined enough to see it influence your behaviours, actions, character and life.

ACHIEVETHEIMPOSSIBLE

THREE MONTHS FROM NOW...

A couple of years ago, I had a dream to write a book about how 100 days could change your life.

That book has since expressed itself in different ways since then, but hey...it may be something that pops its head up again at some stage (watch this space!)

I truly believe this concept can change a life.

3 months doesn't seem like a long time.

How quickly does Christmas come around, how quickly does summer end and how quickly does your child's birthday or your wedding anniversary come around!

It seems just around the corner, but when you look at those three months as containing just under 100 single, individual days...we start to get a scope of the possibilities that 100 days could present.

Ask any pregnant mother entering her final trimester, those last 100 days of her pregnancy, if three months can change a life.

Ask anyone who has received a heart-wrenching diagnosis if three months can change a life.

Ask anyone who has been offered a job opportunity in another country if three months can change a life.

Ask anyone who has met the love of their life if three months can change your life's entire direction.

I know, I know, you've been asking a lot of random people different questions, now it's time to get some answers and apply those to your life.

In a recent study of 96 participants by University College London, Phillippa Lally and her team concluded that it takes 66 days to create a long-term habit.

Exactly two-thirds of one hundred days!

They say habits create behaviours, which in turn develops character, which eventuates in a lifestyle.

One single habit has the power of a flow on effect to change an entire life.

In August of 2017, I made the decision to create the habit of being intentional about what I ate. In the three months following that decision, I lost over 40lbs, I began to love exercising and developed a previously undiscovered sense of self-worth, self-identity and self-confidence.

This was when I began sharing more personal and vulnerable captions to my @peterjbone Instagram community, which has directly resulted in Coaching and Speaking opportunities, as well as this very book you're reading right now!

That one decision to create a habit of healthy eating has changed my life.

What habit can you start today that has been on your heart?

Create space in your day to follow through on that habit and be disciplined enough to see it influence your behaviours, actions, character and life.

In three months, you can be in a completely different space and it can all start today with that one habit.

Focus on today.
Focus on the now.

Do what you can
today to set up your best
possible tomorrow.

Live in the moment
and treasure every single
one of them.

ACHIEVETHEIMPOSSIBLE

STRESSING ABOUT TOMORROW

Focus on the 24 hours in front of you and do what you can to get closer to where you want to be. You've got dreams, goals, desires and ambitions for a big life. I can tell because you've got this very book in your hands!

Firstly, I'm so very grateful for that. I make no exaggerations when I say this book is a dream come true.

Secondly, when we do have these substantial goals for the future, we can all too easily fall into the trap of creating a separation between these illustrious goals for our future and where we are today.

Trust me, I've been there!

And I'm still actively working on it to this day!

There is one key we must master to achieve our long term goals.

Focus on the next 24hrs.

The great thing about the future, despite its incredible potential and power, is that it only comes one moment, one day at a time.

We can get so overwhelmed with our goals for the years ahead that we can paralyse the one moment we can actually do something in...right NOW.

I read a thought today that inspired me to focus on the now...it's a fair read, but definitely worth it!

"You're supposed to be wherever you are; right now, in this moment. Don't fault yourself for not being anywhere other than 'here'. Focus on right now. Focus on today. Make the best out of everything you're already involved with. The future will slowly present itself as you begin to appreciate all that you have and all that you are in this moment. Please don't rush life. Anything's that's meant for you will always be...eventually. Be patient."

- *Reyna Biddy*

Focus on today. Focus on the now. Do what you can today to set up your best possible tomorrow. Live in the moment. And treasure every single one of them.

Life doesn't always happen the way we plan and expect it to unfold.

This is when we have to believe, allow and trust in God's timing.

ACHIEVETHEIMPOSSIBLE

BELIEVE. ALLOW. TRUST.

BELIEVE

Know you've been created for a purpose and been given your dreams, passion and gifting for a reason. Believe in yourself and in your journey ahead.

With this belief in yourself and your journey, comes belief in timing. Where you are right now is where you need to be.

ALLOW

Once we begin developing our belief, our next step is allowing God's timing to occur in our lives. It's way too easy to force something out of its timing and end up blocking your blessing.

Allow where you are to teach and equip you for your journey ahead. Accept what you need to learn and move forward confidently with that knowledge.

TRUST

This is one of my key words for this year. To me, trust is having faith in the unknown. There will be times on this journey to your impossible dreams that you can't see every step of the journey ahead.

These are the times you've got to trust in God's timing of your future steps. He has prepared the way, now He is preparing you for the journey ahead.

This is the shortest chapter in Achieve the Impossible. This is no accident.

I truly believe these three words hold an incredible power and potential to change seasons and circumstances through our perception.

Believe, allow and trust have become the words I find myself repeating over and over in seasons of doubt, fear and uncertainty. Speak these into your situation and apply it to your daily life.

Watch as the expectations and pressures of the unknown slowly release and reveal the way on your path ahead.

BELIEVE, ALLOW and TRUST in God's timing.

Do what you can with what you have in the only moment you can do anything in; this moment right now.

ACHIEVETHEIMPOSSIBLE

THE RIGHT MOMENT

You're never going to be 100% ready and it's never going to be just the right time, but that's the point. It means that every moment is also the right moment. If you want it, you just have to do it.

There's something in your heart.

Something that maybe no one even knows about.

There's a tiny little flame flickering in the depths of you that's been quietly doing its thing, creating a light source within.

As you've watched this flame flicker away, you have a feeling deep down that it's capable of more.

You know it's capable of becoming a fire that can blaze bright within you, creating light and warmth, not just for yourself, but for those around you.

You know there's potential in the flame, but it's not something you wanna smother and extinguish by loading too much fuel on top.

You tell yourself you are waiting for the right time for the flame to grow and build.

Here's the catch...there's never going to be a 'right time'.

Not doing something now because it's not the 'right time' runs by the concept that at some point in the future, this 'right time' will appear.

Unfortunately, we don't have control over the future. We've only got control and influence over one moment...the one we're in right now.

Look at that flickering flame within.

I want to introduce you to your impossible dream.

This flame has incredible potential to burn bright and light your future. We need to take the moment we're in right now and choose to do what we can to fuel the flame.

Does that mean find the biggest log and plonk it on top?

Not at all. One day, your raging furnace will be able to consume that with ease...

But today, we need to tend to the flames and provide fuel that respects the fickle flickering.

Choose to feed your flames with intentional size-appropriate fuel. Start with that small piece of kindling.

It may not seem like much today, but it's what is required to take that flame to the next level.

The timing is never gonna to be 100%.

The harsh reality is our flame isn't going to stay there forever.

Your flame needs fuel. And sometimes that fuel can't wait until it feels like the right time.

Do what you can with what you have in the only moment you can do anything in...this moment right now.

Fuel your flame today and ignite your impossible dream!

IGNITION

Our minds can analyze and prioritize information we've been given from the present moment in the world around us, whilst our instincts can guide and prepare us for the unseen future ahead.

ACHIEVETHEIMPOSSIBLE

TRUST YOUR INSTINCTS

The only moment you have control over is this one you're in now.

We know there will never be a 'right time'.

But how do we know what to do in this moment we have right now?

We've each been blessed with something that can help guide and do life with us.

This gift helps us make decisions, build confidence and points us in the right direction when we can't see clearly ahead. This is called your instinct.

Your instincts have been given to you and dwell in the same neighbourhood as the flame of your impossible dream.

These instincts aren't necessarily loud or over-bearing...they have a quiet confidence about them and somehow they know exactly what we need to do in our next step.

Because they live next door to the flame representing our impossible dreams, they often know things in greater insight and depth than our logic and our brains do.

Our minds can analyze and prioritize information we've been given from the present moment in the world around us, whilst our instincts can guide and prepare us for the unseen future ahead.

There will be times when we have a message from our instincts that really don't make sense to our logical and rational thinking.

Our thinking can't see our flame within. It can feel its warmth and presence, but can't necessarily see what it needs to fuel it for our next step.

This is where instinct kicks in, and from seemingly out of nowhere, can send a message that bypasses the brain and goes straight for our heart.

It could be an instinct to call someone, to take another route or to follow (or not follow) a certain path.

Listen to this instinct.

It often knows more than it lets on.

Trust your instinct and listen to that still small voice that shows you your next step.

The flames of your impossible dream are ignited when your

PASSION meets PREPARATION.

ACHIEVETHEIMPOSSIBLE

WHAT YOU WANT EXISTS

Read that line again. What you want actually exists!

That impossible dream in your heart isn't just there to take up space.

It is a real and tangible force within that can change your entire life if you let it.

Your dream has been given to you for a reason. Fuel that flame, trust in your instincts and be intentional and consistent with each step on the journey ahead.

Want to be a titan of business?

Maybe an award-winning author?

Raise a beautiful family?

Play your music to audiences around the world?

Win the World Cup for your country?

That tiny flickering flame within you exists!

It may not look fierce and powerful now, but the same flame that lights one matchstick can burn an entire forest.

Here's the thing with flames...

You can't just go and buy a box of them.

Flames do not come pre-ignited.

Flames are created when two forces come together.

The flames of your impossible dream are ignited when
your PASSION meets PREPARATION.

That flame within exists. Your dream is possible.

Even if you can't see it yet, that flame is within you, waiting for you to bring
PASSION and PREPARATION together to cause it to IGNITE!

LEVEL UP

It's time to level up!

ACHIEVETHEIMPOSSIBLE

THERE'S ANOTHER LEVEL

This year is the year we are going to our NEXT LEVEL!

Today, we've got a fresh start...a fresh opportunity to tidy up our goals and make this year count!

Whenever you are reading this, be it 2019 or 2049, make this year count!

Let's get a little practical today.

I want you to have a look at your goals for the year.

If you're anything like me, there's a few still on the list that haven't been accomplished as yet.

Where do you go from here?

What do we do with our unfinished goals from last year?

There are two words that sum up this entire concept.

Because I'm writing this, there's a huge chance they are going to at least start with the same letter, or even better, they're gonna rhyme!

'DEFINE and REFINE'

DEFINE

Choose which uncompleted goals you're going to focus on for this coming month. These are ones that are achievable AND you are currently passionate about!

There is no point rushing around, spreading yourself so thin over every single one of your unfinished goals that you accomplish none of them.

Select the top two or three you know you are capable of achieving this month and double down on them!

Write those down. Create a plan. Achieve them.

REFINE

With the two or three monthly goals you're going to focus on, take time to refine what you need to do to achieve them.

If the goal was to complete the manuscript for your book, and you've already smashed out 11 of the 14 chapters, refine your goals to reflect that.

'Write chapters 12-14' is a much tidier goal than 'Finish that damn book that's taking forever!'

Section those up into daily and weekly checkpoints.

 Lastly, and here is where the quote comes in, these final couple of goals are going to demand a personal and intentional 'level up' from you in the next season.

Now's not the time to play safe. Go all-in on these goals whatever time of year you're reading this and be prepared to see major breakthroughs and momentum swings heading into your next season!

Dreaming bigger is a phrase which encapsulates a lifestyle. It's not a results-driven, circumstantial statement, it's a heart position.

ACHIEVETHEIMPOSSIBLE

CREATE THE LIFE YOU WANT

No matter when you're reading this book, now is the perfect time to reflect on the past and look toward the future.

As we look to our goals for the next week, month, year, I challenge you to dream bigger.

Now I know we've probably all heard this a thousand times before and it sounds like the typical motivation cliché, but I really want you to take this to heart.

Dreaming bigger isn't about the numbers.

It's not just a matter of doubling your sales targets or losing more weight.

Dreaming bigger is a phrase with encapsulates a lifestyle. It's not a results-driven, circumstantial statement. It's a heart position.

A heart position that doesn't focus on the final results or outcomes, but rather holistically represents every aspect of life, to encourage us to grow and develop out of the possible and live in the impossible.

Goals are great because they are achievable.

They are results focused and can keep us on track with progress and achievements.

But for your next season, I want you to strip it back down to our inner-self. Let's not just focus on results and measurable outcomes.

Maybe we start to pay a little more attention to things that can't necessarily be measured by numbers...things like passion, purpose, potential and capacity.

Maybe we create a vision for our future with these as the foundation for which we measure our success.

Dreaming bigger isn't about a higher number or a greater challenge. It's about doing what ignites that fire within.

That flame that represents a life's legacy that probably seems impossible.

A dream that you've let flicker away slowly and justified to yourself with outcome and results focused goal-setting progress.

Dream bigger.

Search out the impossible for this year.

Challenge yourself to stretch your capacity and become more and more self-aware of the true desires, passions and purpose of your life here on earth.

The rest of your life starts today.

Look within. Position your heart. Dream bigger.

Your dreams have your name written all over them.

BREAKTHROUGH

Your breakthrough is on its way.

Prepare for the shift.

ACHIEVETHEIMPOSSIBLE

BREAKTHROUGH IS ON ITS WAY!

"There's about to be a shift in your life. Get ready for your blessings. You've been through enough, your breakthrough is on its way. Don't doubt it, just claim it." - Tony Gaskins

Imagine with me, a car driving onto an onramp, preparing to merge onto a Highway. In order to get up to speed, it needs to accelerate and increase revolutions, which allows it to change gears in order to build speed and momentum.

To be honest, for the past couple of years I've felt like I've been driving through the streets, navigating around the twists and turns of life, effectively doing what I've needed to do, but not gaining the distance or speed I'd like.

Now things are changing.

I feel as if those couple of years have prepared me for my journey onto the fast-flowing highway. This onramp is that transition from the bendy streets to the straight highway.

I now know I'm on the onramp.

I've had to accelerate and give more energy into my work, putting in more hours, being more intentional and productive.

It's difficult to maintain these high revs, but you know when those revs are climbing, you're about to shift up a gear.

When you shift up a gear, your revs end up decreasing, but your speed and momentum increase.

If you feel you've been giving it as much as you can, putting in your heart, time and effort...I've got great news. Your shift is about to happen.

Prepare for that shift.

You're heading onto the highway towards your dreams; a place where you can cruise through at a higher speed built with momentum from seasons like this one, where you've put in those extra revs.

Your breakthrough is coming. Prepare for your shift.

You're on your way to your highway.

God is in charge of the plane, the cargo and the timing.

You are in charge of preparing space in your life for the blessings to land.

ACHIEVETHEIMPOSSIBLE

CLEAR THE RUNWAY!

If you've been following my writing for a while, you'll know I love a good ol' picture word/metaphor thingy.

OK, I ADMIT, I AM SLIGHTLY OBSESSED WITH THEM!

This one is one of my absolute favorites, so I have a feeling you'll love it too!

This is one of those metaphors that instantly struck a chord with me...a plane containing our blessings waiting for the runway of our life to be clear.

A plane can't land until the coast is clear. Some of our blessings are stuck in the air because of our environment. There's too much mess on the landing strip.

'Some of our blessings are stuck in the air because of our environment'.

I truly believe your blessing has your name on it.

It is on its way to you as you are reading this right now and contains what you need for today, as well as the next season of your life.

But there's a catch...your blessing needs space to land.

The plane's got YOU as its destination, but if it doesn't have a safe place to land, it's going to have to circle in the air until there's space on the landing strip.

Now here's where we split up the roles in this situation, and to keep it fair, there's one for you and one for God.

God is in charge of the plane, the cargo and the timing.

You are in charge of preparing space in your life for the blessings to land.

It's our responsibility to remove anything that could hinder the plane from a safe landing. And if we're going to stick with the metaphor another level deeper...the bigger the blessing that's coming, the bigger the plane required.

A jumbo jet needs more landing space on the runway than a little Cessna.

The size of your blessing will be influenced by the size of your preparation.

We've got to clear away old mindsets and attitudes that no longer serve us, habits that hold us back and even things that have made their home on your landing strip. These include anything that is taking up space without serving a purpose.

Your blessing is on its way. It's got your name on it.

Prepare space on your landing strip for your next season of blessing!

Just because you don't see a way, doesn't mean God doesn't have a way.

ACHIEVETHEIMPOSSIBLE

THE WAY

You've got your dream...

You know your passion and that is fueling your journey towards your purpose.

Let's start this journey on the road to your impossible dream!

We all know this is gonna be walked out one step at a time. Some of those steps will seem straightforward and natural. Others will need to be more intentional and careful when you traverse over the seasons of rough and rocky terrain.

We know we need to focus on these individual steps, but we also know all too much that it's not just about the practical steps we need to take.

This journey is going to require a relentless and resilient mindset from start to finish. The foundation of this mindset is going to demand trust and faith in the journey ahead.

Why? Because from where you are standing right now, you can't see the entire journey ahead of you.

As uncomfortable as this sounds, it is a part of life!

We're not always going to know the exact details of the way ahead, but we do have access to two very special tour guides, faith and trust.

These beliefs say no matter what lays ahead, I know I'm on the right path because it is aligned to my passion and purpose.

We don't need to know the exact way ahead.

God has already got that planned. You do what you can do and focus on your next step.

The way will reveal itself.

Believe in your dreams. They were given to you for a reason.

ACHIEVETHEIMPOSSIBLE

BELIEVE IN YOUR DREAMS

I truly believe you have been given your dream for a reason. It is no accident that you have your unique set of gifts, talents and abilities. They align perfectly with your passions and purpose, whether you see it now or not.

On one hand, you've got these unique gifts, talents and abilities.

On the other hand, a dream.

A dream that today, could very well seem impossible.

Maybe your dream involves creating; that book, podcast, social channel, album or business that's been on your heart for what seems like a lifetime.

Maybe, like me, you want to start a charity for people the world has seemed to forgotten?

Maybe your dream is relational; finding that person you can share the rest of your life with, raise a family together and inspire the very best in each other.

Maybe your dream is personal; developing yourself to a stage where your change on the inside is finally reflected on the outside, losing that weight you know is holding you back.

Making the decision to persist with healthy lifestyle choices, managing that recurring issue that just keeps on popping up in your life, keeping you from pursuing your greatness.

Maybe your dream is something completely different.

Maybe your dream is something that's so close to your heart, no one knows it but you.

At this very moment, it seems so impossible, you feel it's not even meant to belong to you.

I want you to do something for me. It's something I want you to pause and take a moment to do as one of our first practical tasks together.

I'd like you to think about this dream of yours.

Think about the details of the dream, what your book will smell like, what your album cover will look like, the people your business will interact with and the feeling of reaching the summit of that mountain you've been on the journey of conquering your entire life.

Now, let's think about the person you need to become to achieve this dream.

Together, we will journey, build and develop yourself as an individual to ensure you're operating at your absolute best. That's what your dream requires, so that's what we'll be focusing on.

You've got your dream. Strap yourself and your dream in nice and tight, because we're about to embark on a journey to make that 'impossible' dream a reality.

From the moment I started @achievetheimpossible in Dec 2013, I knew my life's purpose and mission was to support people to achieve (wait for it...) their impossible dream.

For those of you who are thinking 'Pete, wait! I don't have a dream just yet!' Don't worry! I've got good news.

By spending time everyday cultivating and developing your mindset, thoughts and beliefs surrounding your dream, you will find your passions and purpose will slowly start to reveal themselves, which could lead you straight to your impossible dream.

RELAX

The hustle is over-rated!

ACHIEVETHEIMPOSSIBLE

OVER-RATED HUSTLE

"Destroy the idea that you have to be constantly working or grinding in order to be successful. Embrace the concept that rest, recovery and reflection are essential parts of the progress towards a successful and ultimately happy life." - Jonah Hill

The hustle is over-rated!

I'm sure you've heard more than enough of your fair share of the word 'hustle' on any Instagram account even slightly featuring a motivational flavor.

It's one of those words that gets a heck of a lot of air-time and does get some pretty glorified responses.

While there is an absolute time and season to 'hustle' and put work first, there is also this little thing called 'balance' that is necessary for a life lived to its highest potential over the long-term.

We can tend to glorify the grind and hustle so much that we can be guilty of accepting an un-balanced and ultimately unsustainable life and the accompanying lifestyle.

If you love picture words like me (this far through the book, you really should by now!), here's one just for you.

The hustle and grind are like the glorified accelerator pedal of a race car. It gets you going and moving off the start line and is obviously the one thing that builds speed and momentum.

If our life was raced in a perfectly straight line, the hustle and grind of an accelerator pedal is all we would need, right?!

Unfortunately, life is never going to be just a straight run.

The track of life brings twists and turns, up-hills, down-hills, curves and even the odd hairpin corner thrown in there.

If we didn't take our foot off the gas or use the brake, our lives would quickly spin out of control when navigating one of these turns at full speed.

This is where the true balance of the brake pedal comes in.

There will be times when we have no choice but to resort to the brakes in order to navigate the inevitable bends and curves ahead.

Yes, the hustle and grind is necessary to get around the track, and at certain times, put that pedal to the metal!

But within a balanced and sustainable long-term life...rest, recovery and reflection are essential to keep us from spinning out of control.

You've got access to both pedals, hustle and rest.

Don't be afraid to use either when the time is right and the situations require a change of pace. What pedal do you need to be focused on using more of today?

Maybe you're not getting what you want because it's not meant for you.

ACHIEVETHEIMPOSSIBLE

STOP COMPETING. RELAX.

I've been exploring this thought over the past few days as it's something that jumped out at me and got me thinking.

We can get so caught up in striving for things we think are for us and fighting certain battles, that in all honesty, are actually not ours to fight.

It's way too easy to strive after things that are not actually meant for us in the first place; the relationship, the promotion you've always assumed would change your life, the new house, new town or new country.

When we are striving for things that are not meant to be, we become frustrated. First of all, we become frustrated because deep down, because we know this one change in environment is not going to actually solve our life's problems.

That one person you're desperate to be in a relationship with who you think will magically make you feel complete, that pay rise you think will solve all financial struggles, that new town to escape the drama within your community.

These may put a band-aid on a wound, but they're not going to heal what's broken inside.

Secondly, we become frustrated because nothing just seems to click; house contracts are falling through, people are acting strange and unpredictable out of their character, Ben from accounts got the promotion instead of you!

Maybe you're not getting what you want because it's not meant for you.

Focus on developing yourself, your relationship with God and listening to that still, small voice within that says everything will work out.

Does this give us free license to sit back and wait for everything to come our way? Absolutely not. I think it means letting go of your expectations of the future and what you think should happen, and focus on today and what actually is happening.

Maybe the reason you haven't gotten what is meant for you yet is because you're simply not ready for it.

Stop stressing over what you can't control and focus on what you can; yourself, your actions and your reactions.

Whether you can feel it or not, you've been given your own lane for the journey ahead.

ACHIEVETHEIMPOSSIBLE

STAYING IN YOUR LANE

This lane takes you to every checkpoint you need to visit on the journey to your impossible dream.

Your lane isn't going to be perfectly straight...no one's is.

Your lane will have twists and turns, unexpected climbs, potholes and slippery surfaces.

But your lane will also have graceful downhill sections where your hard work pays off as you glide towards your destination.

When you are positioned on your lane, you don't need to worry about the uphills and challenges, and you also don't need to feel guilty for the downhill sections. Your lane is YOUR lane for a reason. That means every up and down, twist and turn has a purpose behind it.

You don't need to strive and stress about what you're facing. All you need to focus on is staying in your lane and progressing each and every day towards your destination.

Staying in your lane is so peaceful.

This doesn't mean you won't have challenges, it means that you're equipped to handle every uphill because you are never given a section of road you can't handle.

Stay in your lane...focus on what's yours and enjoy the journey!

SUCCESS

Embrace change. It's the process we experience on the road to becoming all we are called to be.

ACHIEVETHEIMPOSSIBLE

EMBRACE CHANGE

Change is the catalyst of success.

We all know that in order to grow, we must experience change. Change is never as easy and simple as it seems.

Change can often be uncomfortable, painful and frightening. But don't despair. I have good news.

Underneath the surface of these feelings, change is building and creating a solid foundation for future growth.

Let's jump into another metaphor (you're getting the picture of how much much I love them by now!)

Get your hard hat and work boots on, and come join me on the construction site.

Before a building starts construction, its foundations must be strong and be able to withstand the pressure that will come upon it in the coming season of vertical growth.

In order to set a strong foundation, the ground must be broken and dug up, and guess what?!

The bigger the planned structure, the more intensive the earthworks.

This change under the surface is essential.

The foundations of grass, dirt and earth must be reinforced with the stronger substances of concrete and steel. Space under the surface needs to be cleared in order for the reinforced substances to be positioned for future construction.

The same thing happens in our lives.

Change and growth require areas of our lives to be shaken up, dug out and space to be cleared in order for the stronger, more resilient and reliable foundations to be laid.

When you're going through this time of change, don't focus on what is happening in the shake-up.

Instead, choose to focus on the future structure that can now be built because of your stronger foundations.

Change is essential.

Change is active growth.

Change prepares you to achieve your 'impossible' dreams.

Embrace change. It's the process we experience on the road to becoming all we are called to be.

If you feel you're being tested, challenged and things are rubbing the shine and exterior coat of protection off you, it's very likely you're being prepared for a brand new fresh coat of blessings!

ACHIEVETHEIMPOSSIBLE

TRUST IN THE PAINTER

Success and failure are on the very same road.

There have been times in my life when I've encountered pot holes, uneven slippery surfaces and difficult obstacles on the road to my dreams. These unexpected challenges can catch you off-guard.

During these times where the road isn't as smooth as we thought it would be, the thoughts of fear and doubt can start to creep in.

'It shouldn't be this hard.'

'This obviously isn't the road for me.'

'If God had wanted me to have it, He wouldn't be putting me though this.'

The times when the journey is challenging and difficult are preparing you for the blessings ahead.

Before you put a fresh coat of paint on a wall, you've got to use sand-paper to prepare the wall for its next season of life.

Sanding down the walls has a two-fold purpose.

First, it removes any ridges or uneven surfaces that have built up on what was on the wall previously from the last coat of paint.

Secondly, and this is the point I really want to focus on...sanding the previous coat of paint gives the fresh coat something to adhere to.

If you apply a fresh coat of paint directly onto an old coat, the paint won't have have the substance to stick to.

I feel the same for our journey of life.

There will be times when we feel as if we're being sanded and our outer layer of shine is being roughed up.

During the process, this feels awful.

But the painter knows the purpose to the paper.

If you feel you're being tested, challenged and things are rubbing the shine and exterior coat of protection off you, it's very likely you're being prepared for a brand new fresh coat of blessings!

Trust in the painter.

The same wall that is getting roughed up now is the same wall that is about to get a fresh coat of paint.

The difference? Time and progress.

Stick to the road you truly believe is yours.

It may feel like you're going through a season of being roughed up by failure, but hang in there and stay strong!

Your fresh coat of paint and blessings are on their way!

BE POSITIVE

Being positive ensures YOU are okay, despite the circumstances around you.

ACHIEVETHEIMPOSSIBLE

THE CHOICE

Being positive is a choice we make.

Unfortunately, it's not a decision we make once and guaranteed to make everything in our lives bright and cheery, overflowing with rainbows and unicorns.

This decision to be positive must be made everyday, and then subsequent numerous times throughout that day.

You see, we live in a world where we are presented with negative news, images, stories and accounts almost everywhere we look.

Being positive isn't going to instantly fix world peace, hunger, racism, hate and violence.

But here's what being positive does do...

Being positive ensures that you have faith in a brighter tomorrow, a gratefulness for where you are today and who you have surrounding you.

Being positive ensures that no matter what is happening around you, you are focused on the beauty of our world.

That quiet, peaceful and still beauty can easily be flooded and overwhelmed by the noise of the world events happening all around us.

Being positive doesn't guarantee these things will all work out perfectly and be okay. It ensures YOU will be okay.

Despite what's going on in your world, make the decision to be positive.

Look at the bright side of the situations you're in...

Instead of seeing a stressful mortgage payment,
be grateful you've got a place to stay.

Instead of hearing your noisy kids who won't go to bed,
be grateful you've been blessed with them.

Instead of hating your boss, be thankful you've got a job.

Being positive ensures YOU are okay despite the circumstances around you.

"An entire sea of water can't sink a ship unless it gets inside the ship. Similarly, the negativity of the world can't put you down unless you allow it to get inside you." - *Goi Nasu*

You may not be where you want to be.

But you're not where you were.

That is PROGRESS.

Be proud of where you are today.

ACHIEVETHEIMPOSSIBLE

PURPOSE OF PROGRESS

We all have our dreams, ambitions, hope and desires for the future.

You want to start that business, become financially free, make your dream team, create that masterpiece you know you're capable of, write the book that's been on your heart for years or lose that weight that's been holding you back from being the person you know you truly are.

These dreams have been placed inside of you for a reason. They are not an accident. We need that dream to fuel our determination and the internal drive to get there.

The thing about 'impossible' dreams is they don't happen overnight. Every dream requires a process and that process can take a heck of a long time and will more than likely involve blood, sweat and tears.

There will be days you feel overwhelmed and outnumbered by the stress, anxiety and worry that attaches itself to the unknown.

But there there will also be days where things just seem to click and you push through barriers and obstacles that were holding you back.

Setbacks and breakthroughs have one thing in common; they reflect progress.

Coming across a setback three months into your journey means you've progressed three months and now you are encountering fresh things you haven't had to encounter for those past three months.

Setbacks are the natural result of progress!

In the same way, breakthroughs reflect progress also.

Breakthroughs are just so much more fun than setbacks!

Through your journey, amidst the setbacks and breakthroughs, keep focused on that one word, PROGRESS.

That is all you need to focus on.

You may not be where you want to be.

But you're not where you were.

That is PROGRESS.

Be proud of where you are today.

Let's live life pursuing 100%

ACHIEVETHEIMPOSSIBLE

GIVING IT 100%

Giving it 100%...

Imagine you had a LIVE percentage tracker on your life 24/7. This percentage tracker constantly evaluated your level of effort and effectiveness towards every single thing you do, every minute of every day.

Does it already sound daunting?

Bear with me as I flesh this idea out. Imagine you were being rated from 0% - 100% in terms of your effectiveness in using your time and energy to its greatest possible potential.

You're sitting on the highway on your way to work...are you listening to the same four songs on the radio, yelling at every second car in traffic and counting down the minutes before you get trapped in your office for the next 8hrs? Sound familiar?

What do you think you would you operating at?

I'd imagine it would be close to 0%. You're doing the bare minimum...getting your butt to work.

Now let's flip the coin.

You're sitting on the highway on your way to work.

You make the decision to put on an inspiring and equipping podcast, you are being intentional about sharing a smile with the person next to you and you're grateful for the opportunity to have a job so your family have a roof over their heads and food on the table.

What do you think you'd you operating at this time?

I'd be confident to say it would be much closer to 100%.

The cool thing is it's honestly not that difficult to make subtle changes to slide up the scale and improve your percentage from 0% to 100%.

Those small simple changes in our daily routine over a consistent period of time, result in huge improvement down the road.

Let's start focusing on those small daily habits that bring our percentage tracker closer to 100%. Let's use our time wisely and do everything we can to dedicate our lives to giving everything we do our very best.

Today, I want you to choose an area of your life that you could get closer to 100% on.

Maybe it's a time of the day, a part of your routine or maybe a role or project you're working on. Whatever it is, create a plan to make the most of that time.

Let's start living a life pursuing 100%.

Whether it be working, resting or playing. It sows the seeds of tomorrow.

You're on this path
for a reason.

You're capable of
completing it.

You've come this far,
see it through.

ACHIEVETHEIMPOSSIBLE

STAY STRONG

The journey towards your impossible dream is an interesting one.

There'll be times when you're pumped full of adrenalin, bashing down every obstacle that comes your way.

There will be times you're cruising on a nice downhill slope, enjoying the scenery and wondering why it took you this long to convince yourself to get here!

Then, plain and simply, there'll be times when things are difficult.

Just like my climb recently up a little mountain by my home on the Sunshine Coast of Australia.

I started out full of energy, pumped for the adventure ahead...then 5 minutes into the usually very achievable rocky steps, my legs started really feeling it.

The adrenalin gave way to frustration, to fear and to my quickly draining self-belief in my fitness.

I continued one painful step at a time.

I wasn't going the pace I normally would, but knew this mountain could be conquered one slow step at a time.

As I slowly neared the end of the steps, my legs were burning, my heart pounding and my mindset weakening. Two quiet words burst through my pain...

'Stay strong'

I'm pretty sure I've never said this going up the mountain before, but it seemed fitting.

As I climbed one step at a time, 'stay strong' became my repeated mantra...

After the season of pain and intentional mindset building, I reached the summit of the mountain and cruised my way back down.

There is such an incredibly untapped power within our self-belief and mindset, which shapes our self-talk.

On your journey towards your impossible dream, I can almost guarantee you'll be faced with steps that seem too difficult, too challenging, too much to conquer.

Remember those two words...stay strong.

You're on this path for a reason.

You're capable of completing it.

You've come this far, see it through.

If you've found yourself in a situation you can't control, focus your perspective on what you do have control over, yourself and your response.

ACHIEVETHEIMPOSSIBLE

FOCUS ON THE POSITIVE!

Every time we're faced with a situation, we have one of two choices. Both of those are determined and directly influenced by one word...'Perspective'; how we see the situation we've currently found ourselves in.

Now our first option is often our default reaction...sit and dwell over the negative aspects and begin to throw blame towards the factors which are usually out of our control.

This can feel justified, but really, if we're being completely honest with ourselves... it's pretty much just an adult version of a temper-tantrum.

There's a quote by Edwin Louis Cole which I absolutely love that represents this perfectly...

"You don't drown by falling in the water. You drown by staying there."

When you find yourself in a situation that causes stress, fear, doubt and anxiety... don't stay in it.

If you've fallen overboard, keep your head up and start swimming back to safety.

YOUR FIRST STEP is a perspective shift.

Have a look at the situation and reflect on the way you are viewing what's happening right now. Chances are this is a temporary situation that, if we're honest, isn't ideal, but is a part of life, so we've gotta move on and deal with it.

One way I find useful to regain perspective is to take a mental step back and see the big picture.

See this moment through the lens of our future.

Is this really going to matter in a week, a month, a year...even ten years from now?

Not usually, so get your head out of the water, and focus on where you need to swim.

YOUR SECOND STEP is to take action and start swimming!

It says it all right here.

'Be grateful and focus on the positive'

The most powerful way for me to experience gratitude in my life is to write the things I'm grateful for down on paper.

Gratitude is said to be one of our most influential feelings and emotions. Displaying a sense of gratitude for the things you have now can unlock the future blessings stored up for you.

Write down three things you're grateful for.

A useful technique to help you start is to look around you.

The roof over your head, your washing machine, your table, your computer, your son, your husband.

You can definitely show gratitude for things that are intangible i.e. your job, your health, your passions, etc etc, but I prefer to list things that I can see, touch and connect with on a physical level.

If you've found yourself in a situation you can't control, focus your perspective on what you do have control over...yourself and your response.

Use the power of gratitude to take action and do what's in your control to do to get you back on the boat, sailing towards your dreams!

All we have is each moment.

Choose to make the most of it.

ACHIEVETHEIMPOSSIBLE

THE PRESENT MOMENT

I'm not where I want to be, but I'm also not where I used to be...I'm exactly where I need to be in this present moment.

We're changing it up a little with this final chapter of 'Achieve the Impossible'!

I won't be sharing a metaphor or conjuring up a picture word, we're going with a story. A true story! And there is no truer story than one that has literally just happened to me a couple of months ago! I remember it like it was yesterday.

As I walked along the beach, I stared at a blank note document on my phone, thinking about the chapter i was to write today (I get most of my writing inspiration from the beach!)

I knew I wanted to talk about appreciating each and every single moment, but my four initial attempts at the opening line proved it would be a little trickier than I anticipated.

My frustration was building as I was wondered what to write. This is often when the breakthrough comes...and that exactly what happened.

As I looked down at my feet, the last trickles of waves were touching the sand before retreating back to their home. I was walking on the border between sand and sea.

Something struggling on the wet sand caught my attention. A tiny orange and black moth fluttered hopelessly in the sand.

I continued walking past...

You know those moments when something grips your heart and doesn't let go? This was one of those.

No more than 6 steps past, I knew I had to turn around to see what I could do to help this colourful creature.

As I approached, I saw another wave approaching, heading straight for the flailing moth.

In a superhero-to-the-bugs kinda way, I swooped down and picked up the moth just split seconds before that wave rolled in and immersed the sand.

I placed the damp moth on my dry wrist.

It paused...stunned by the moment.

Then the moment of truth. He flapped his first flap of freedom. A few more flaps and the little guy was ready for take-off!

As he flew off into the distance, my heart turned to my mind and said 'Well done Pete. We did good.'

Then here we are in this proceeding moment right now.

I find myself writing about appreciating the exact thing I almost took for granted.

Life and death were decided in that moment.

Stalling on that moment would've ended the life of the moth I had the chance to save.

You may not be a superhero to a moth like me, but we've all been given a moment.

A moment where we choose to give life to where we are and who we are with in the present.

Each moment we are in has two bordering neighbours.

The past and the future.

We can choose to focus on what we've done and where we've been in the past.

Or we can focus on the opposite side of the spectrum and look solely to the future...where we are going and how we're getting there.

Reflecting on the past is a powerful learning tool. Planning for the future can inspire greatness within.

But like my moment this morning, I'm going to invest my time focusing on the present much more.

I'm not where I want to be, but I'm also not where I used to be...I'm exactly where I need to be in this present moment.

I am making the decision to focus on the now. I know that little moth is grateful I am. The future will come in its time, the past has gone.

All we have is each moment.

Choose to make the most of it.

Life is lived in moments. These moments hold the potential of the impossible. Decide today that you are becoming the person your dream needs you to be and achieve your impossible!

EPILOGUE

First of all, before we get into the final goodbyes of this book, let me say something to you, person to person, writer to reader.

Ironically, words cannot explain how truly grateful I am you're reading this right now. The fact you're holding my first ever physical, actual real-life book with actual real-life paper pages is a dream come true for me.

This book (in case you haven't guessed it yet) is about achieving the impossible.

In reading it, I hope and trust that you will be inspired, challenged and equipped to achieve your own impossible dreams. In a crazy twist of fate, almost like it's written that way, by you holding the book right now, you have helped me achieve my impossible.

This book is a physical manifestation of a dream becoming a reality.

In the same way you've helped me achieve my impossible, my heart's desire is to be right beside you on the journey to you achieving your impossible dream. This is where the book comes in.

I can't be with each and every single one of you every single day, but my words can.

I can't spend a rainy morning drinking coffee with you, but my words can.

I can't be sitting on your bedside table at night, but my words can.

This book isn't a read through once and put on the shelf kind of book.

I've written this book to be a part of your daily life. To be with you on this journey in pursuit of your impossible is the purpose behind what you're holding right now. A book in which you can turn to when you're needing that touch of inspiration as you pursue your impossible dream.

The pages of this book aren't designed to look perfect and pristine.

They are for you to highlight, write over, underline and scribble inspiration through. Take out one line as your daily inspiration, or use an entire chapter as the hope you're holding onto for the week. No matter how you do it, make the words your own, apply them to your life where you're at, in whatever you may be doing.

This book isn't meant to be kept a secret from the world.

Share it with your friends, your family, with anyone alongside you on the journey to achieving your impossible. Talk about it, think about it, write your own notes and takeaway points from it. This book is yours, but the inspiration is for everyone.

Although the themes and principles can cater to many scenarios, apply them to your individual situation and season. They aren't just words on a page from a guy in Australia you found on Instagram. They are sparks to ignite a flame within. Read them, understand them and apply them.

Your impossible dream is waiting for you. Your path has been set out before you. The person you're capable of becoming is right in front of you, arms stretched wide, desperate for you to step into the possibility of your untapped potential and capacity.

Your world needs you to achieve your impossible dream.

Your world needs you to become the person your impossible dream requires you to be. You have been given it because you are truly capable of achieving it. Own it. Believe it. Pursue it.

Take your next step on the journey to achieving your impossible dream.

Pete

First of all, I'd like to thank my Dad, Johnny Bone - your legacy lives on through every life that comes into contact with Achieve the Impossible, including this book. I love you and miss you.

Thank you to God for giving me a purpose that builds others. and to my family and friends who have supported me on this journey.

Last but definitely not least, a massive thank you to YOU!

You are the one I've written this for, with the hope I can play a small part in inspiring you to achieve your impossible.

I trust and pray the words you've read and will hopefully read through time and time again will inspire, challenge and equip you. Not just today, but with every single step you take on the journey to achieving your impossible dream.

Achieve the Impossible.

Peter J. Bone

———————————————

Peter J Bone is a Social Media Coach, Writer, and Content Creator who lives in the tropical paradise of Noosa, Australia.

His purpose and mission is to inspire people to achieve their impossible dream.

With an unrelenting passion to inspire, challenge and equip people to achieve their impossible dreams, he has grown an online Instagram community of over one million people who are in pursuit of their impossible dreams.

As a result of this influence, experience and Instagram specific knowledge, he now has the opportunity to Coach and Consult Businesses and Entrepreneurs on their Instagram presences all the way from London to New York, as well as professional athletes in Australia and NZ.

His dream is that he could share words and content that would pierce the reality of what's possible and encourage people around the world to pursue their God-given dreams and achieve their impossible.

@peterjbone

@achievetheimpossible

peterjbone.com

achievetheimpossible.com